Dedication
For Pauline and the girls
and Mum and Dad

Cover and back photographs by Anton Corbijn

Inside jacket front and back photographs by Peter Anderson

A lot of people helped me with this book and to them I am particularly grateful. It's not necessary to compile a list because they all know who they are. Thank you.

First published in 1981 by Eel Pie Publishing Limited, 45, Broadwick Street, London W1V 1FS

© Tony Stewart 1981

ISBN 0 906008 47 6

Printed and bound in Great Britain by R. J. Acford, Industrial Estate, Chichester, Sussex.

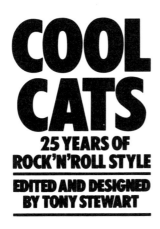

COOL CATS
25 YEARS OF ROCK'N'ROLL STYLE
EDITED AND DESIGNED BY TONY STEWART

SPECIAL PHOTOGRAPHY:
ANTON CORBIJN AND PETER ANDERSON
RESEARCH: MURIEL ROE

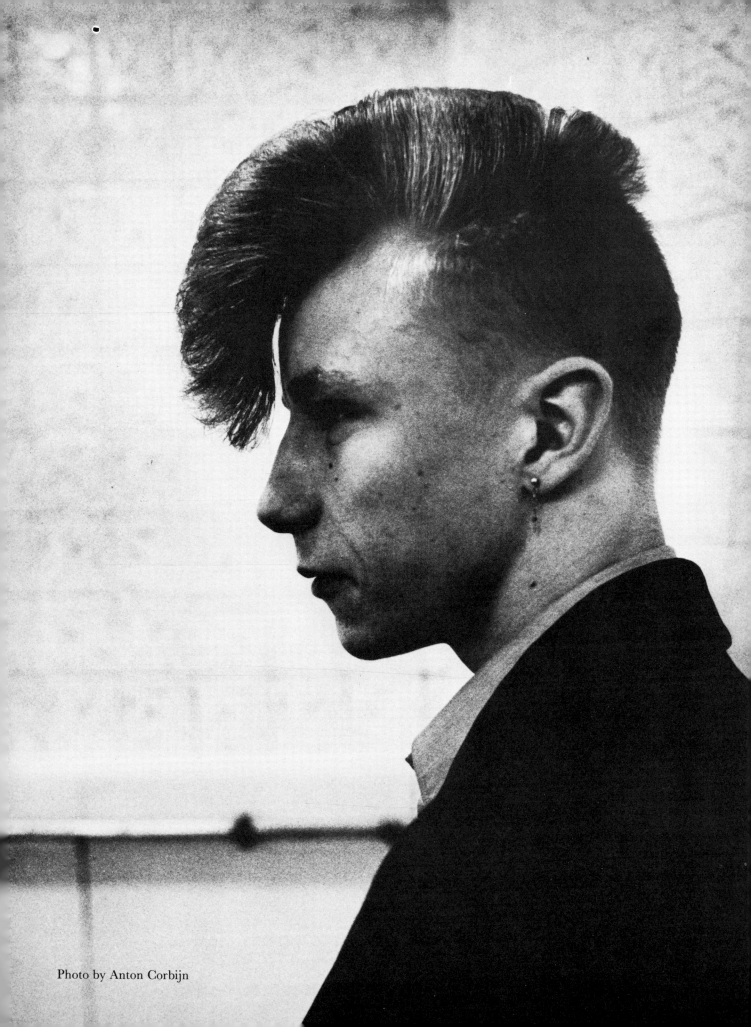

Photo by Anton Corbijn

Introduction
PUTTING ON THE STYLE
By Tony Stewart

When I was still at junior school I clearly remember the outrage in our parochial community when our next-door neighbour's son became a Teddy boy.

His name was Fred and he worked at the Rowntree's factory in York. Fred had fair hair that he greased with Brylcream and swept back into a quiff and duck's arse. He wore long jackets, drainpipe jeans and brothel creepers, and used to do naughty things with local girls in his old black Austin.

Everybody used to talk about Fred: he'd razored a bloke in a pub one day; he got sacked from his last job because he wore purple socks; he'd put a bun in Sally's oven. When he drove home pissed on a Saturday night, hiccupping as much as his old Austin, you could see the curtains in the street move. Then Fred had to do his National Service, and because he lived next door to me, I went in to see him before he left. I was only a kid but he didn't mind me being in the front bedroom while he packed his battered brown suitcase. It wasn't in Fred's nature to be miserable, so he kept joking about what he'd do in the army, what a great time he'd have. He'd got rid of the Austin and his Dad was going to drive him into York to catch the train. I was really sad that Fred was going because he was . . . well, different. And when he suddenly took up his battered acoustic guitar that he'd painted yellow and told me I could have it, he took on a very special meaning.

Fred was my first rock 'n' roll hero.

Of course there have been many since, and hopefully many more to come, and I can't honestly say that Fred was the inspiration for *Cool Cats*. Certainly he's played a part in these pages because I've never subscribed to the theory that rock 'n' roll is only created by the singers and the groups; it's a result of *all* the people involved.

The idea behind this book was to show how rock 'n' roll style got off the street onto the stage and back again.

Another thing about Fred is that all the ridiculous stories weren't based on a shred of fact, but were inspired by his appearance. And that has been one of the most striking qualities of rock – that an image, a style, can create more of a reaction, more controversy than the music. Rock 'n' roll is a visual culture. The look is just as important as the noise.

There were a lot of people like Fred (and there still are). He was there in the '50s. It's a decade that has never ended, and it's also when the '80s began. The styles of 25 years ago have never died, they've just gone out of fashion. Talk of 'revival' is bullshit. It's absurd to think that it's even possible to pull down the shutters on an era: good rock 'n' roll has such a devastating effect that it is never forgotten.

Really the music and the look create The Image – and yet whenever there has been a 'definitive' study of the culture, the emphasis has invariably been on a critical analysis of the music. In the '50s, the pop writers condemned the provocative physical gyrations of Elvis and Cliff, yet invariably sought justification for this 'moralistic' attack in their music. In the '60s umpteen millions of words were written about Beatlemania when one picture would have told the story. And when in the '70s the British rock press moved up market intellectually in a bid to achieve equal status with their American counterparts, the various rock and pop phenomena were analysed in a dirge of grey type rather than a series of self-explanatory pictures.

Rock 'n' roll style is visual, a combination of dress, attitude

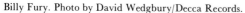

Billy Fury. Photo by David Wedgbury/Decca Records.

Paul Weller.

and music. And that's the formula that firms were quick to appreciate in the '60s. With The Beatles came a mass merchandising boom: the fans have always wanted to imitate the stars and supporters' colours were nothing new to teen culture. Beatle boots, jackets and wigs became big business, and the ragtrade quickly adopted the role previously played by Tin Pan Alley. So, youth's love of primal rhythms and sexual imagery – often the essence of rock 'n' roll – was exploited and marketed by a variety of buck-making entrepreneurs. T-shirts, badges, posters, hats, socks, scarves, shoes and trousers have all been produced to service teenage cults.

Inevitably, some sharp entrepreneur would attempt to 'manufacture' a band as a front for a commercial enterprise. Probably the one person who has managed that is Malcolm McLaren – one time manager of The New York Dolls, The Sex Pistols and Bow Wow Wow. With the Pistols he provided a focus for a movement of rebellion and resentment: a look of scrap metal and torn rags to represent cultural anarchy. With that contribution made to the iconoclastic '70s, in the '80s he dreamed up Bow Wow Wow – basically a clothes horse for McLaren and his associate Vivienne Westwood's '81 fashion collection. It was a shrewd move to create your own performing models. And with the help of some easily manipulated media mannequins, McLaren launched national sensations more related to fashion than style.

It was a result of these events that the idea for *Cool Cats* came about: to trace and illustrate the various trends and

show the power of visual impact rather than musical content.

My initial idea was to design a book around six sections, none of which would be tied to any one period. To me The Stray Cats belonged as much to the '50s as they did the '80s; Bill Haley's influence spanned 25 years from 'Rock Around The Clock' to his death in 1981. Mod, supposedly a '60s trend, re-emerged in the '70s; psychedelia became an '80s phenomenon, not just a '60s happening. Teddy boys swanked through 25 years; and rockabilly is very much an '50s style that never really found its moment until the '80s, despite Hank Mizell.

Then each section had to have a commentary that reflected this new interpretation, that took a different view of a well-known subject. It wasn't hard to decide who I should ask to write the chapters: the people from *New Musical Express* – Cynthia Rose, Paul Morley and Paul Du Noyer – are three of my favourite writers, distinctive for their individual styles and enthusiasm for the subject.

I wanted Cynthia to write Girlstyle after reading her article in *Harpers And Queen* called 'Rock Around The Frock', but suggested her chapter for *Cool Cats* should take a different angle and broader scope, and be aimed specifically at a rock audience.

Paul Morley, I knew, wanted to write an article on Glam that would completely overthrow the tired concepts of Glamrock and offer a new interpretation of such a broad, important and influential facet of rock style.

Paul Du Noyer was a '70s teenager; he grew up with the

6

August Darnell.

Lux Interior. All three photos by Anton Corbijn.

music and style and was keen to do an article that combined his personal experiences with his professional knowledge of a most bizarre and disruptive decade.

Ian Dury is a performer and stylist I admire immensely, and he seemed the right choice to write the '50s chapter. It's a series of scenarios, evocative and often extremely personal, that recreate wonderfully his early teen life as the Upminster Kid. If his narrative was a set of lyrics, they would make a terrific LP. Ian also got into the atmosphere of the whole venture, and when we went out to his wife's home to do a photo session with the Bill Haley poster featured on the cover, he played out the part dramatically with the chewing gum, shades, donkey jacket and symbolic kiss curl.

Paul Weller too, engrossed himself in the atmosphere and attitudes of the '60s for his chapter. I remember when he and I first met to discuss the project he was recording in the Polydor Studios in London. He has never tried to deny his fascination with '60s culture, even if he has invariably been unable to articulate his ideas in pop paper interviews, and it was ironic that the demo track he should play me that day was 'Start'. Based quite blatantly on The Beatles' 'Taxman', it was a good omen for a '60s article written from an '80s perspective. Paul Weller is as much the eternal mod as Pete Townshend.

Much of this book was made possible by the work and ideas of two photographers – Anton Corbijn and Peter Anderson. The photographic research was the most enjoyable experience of the book: not only did Anton and Peter offer

me access to their own files and innumerable photography books, but I also visited the libraries of Dezo Hoffman, David Wedgbury and Ray Stevenson. For me it was a particularly exciting task to search through Beatles and Small Faces pictures and begin to appreciate the characters of the artists involved by seeing not only some 'classic' shots but the complete session from which those famous photographs came.

Looking at Stevenson's hundreds of contact sheets was no less a revelation. In the mid '70s Ray worked with The Sex Pistols and was one of the few photographers who'd regularly visit the London punk clubs – the Roxy, the Marquee, the Nashville and the 100 Club – little realising that five years later he alone would have almost the complete story of one of the most explosive youth movements in rock 'n' roll's history.

"It's like letting you read my diary," he told me one day, half-embarrassed.

Cool Cats isn't a fashion book, and nor is it intended to be an illustrated history of rock 'n' roll. It is purely a personal view of style, one that projects image and attitudes, paradoxes and coincidences, through hair, clothes, manner and posing. There are no excuses for the omissions; just because it existed in rock doesn't mean to say it's stylish or that it played an essential part in the development of style.

For too long the look has been secondary to the word. *Cool Cats* reverses tradition and presents the pictorial story of rock 'n' roll style.

7

Jerry Lee Lewis   Photo by Dezo Hoffman

The Fifties
RAZORS OUT AT ROCK RIOT
By Ian Dury

The sideburns are coming on: less bum fluff, more little black ones. Anzora white preparation for the haircut. Water on first – sides only if the grapes look healthy. Dreadful randolphs round the corners of the mouth. Mr and Mrs Bates and their little son Master Bates. Except on rare occasions. Still warmly dripping down the leg of my memory. They were doing the creep: some things happen by accident in the dark.

Enough dough for two coffees, five weights possible bus ride and disc Jockey Jamboree.

Grey worsted trousers with 12″ bottoms done on my mum's hand-drive singer, yellow and black check shirt and horrible one button jacket bought by mistake in Romford market when the geezer put his arm across the door and convinced me that pale green cardboard was just as smart as grey donegal tweed with little coloured speckles in it which is what I really wanted and still have yearnings about. I hated that jacket. It made me feel sick sometimes. I bought a black denim rock suit with white stitching from a melody maker postal advert six months later, but until then all I had was scholastic apparel or that fucking slimy jacket. Also I pretended that my feet were not involved since the health service didn't make clubmans and still don't, but at least these days they try.

Bowl down waldegrave turn right at hall lane past upminster station and the international stores where once waiting for a bus Harris leant against the front window which, unbeknownst to him, had been removed for the hot day and sent the pyramids of beans and soup tins crashing and rolling accompanied by screams of delight down the hill. One got as far as Bell Corner. Turn left down St Marys lane. Meet Emmett of american merchant seaman attire and disposition. Good cloth Simon. Chuz chuz you bastard. Get down the regent. Hallo queenie two coffees please. Give me fourpence you cunt; Quick; that cunt Hargreaves is slinging all his wedge in the jukebox; go and press great balls of fire for him. Alright you cunt.

Too late. He's stuck it all on Bill Haley.

Never mind never mind: Razzle Dazzle, Mambo Rock, Hot Dog Buddy buddy Coming through the Rye. Blackboard Jungle was a great film and Bill Haley's best record, Rock around the clock was on the soundtrack. Juvenile delinquency and rock 'n' roll: it was combination punches to the head and heart. Vic Morrow was the first of a long line of captain sensibles and Big Bill Haley was the first cuckoo of spring.

Even then he was old and plump with a comical haircut and a free-form eye, and for these reasons was nobody's idea of a jeepster. His voice was woefully dull neuter alto; his music had a strong backbone beat, plus the great saxophone playing of Rudy Pompelli, but was little more than cold slick country clockwork. The comets were good players who seemed glad to have escaped from some roadhouse and they rolled about in their tuxedos with feigned glee. Bill was obviously a lovely geezer because the band stayed together (playing the same set) for over a quarter of a century, and now him and Rudy are dead, rock around the clock will always be their monument.

His rise to enormous fame stemmed partly from his links with blackboard jungle and also two rock'n'roll films in which he starred. Before Little Richard and Elvis Presley's tuttis of the frutti completely eclipsed the old buzzard a year later, he was top man in the popularity stakes and champion of the teds who danced in the cinema aisles and embarked on

1950s Tommy Steele models prototype British quiff. Photo by Dagens Bild.

1950s Bill Haley, kiss curl and grin and guitar. All he ever needed. Photo courtesy of Decca Records.

increasingly riotous orgies of destruction whenever Don't knock the Rock came to town. And though his music was not revolutionary in any sense, everyone associated it with having a bloody good time. Gee we're gonna miss you, everybody sends their love.

It was films that gave everybody a chance to congregate. Before there were many concerts. Meat for Cats with the Ted Heath orch and Terry Dene, or the Marty Wilde Wee Willie Harris Rory 'shakes' Blackwell package didn't happen till late '57 and early '58 and before the television had got us by the goolies, Sunday afternoon was when we used to sit round the big screen, telling jokes singing songs and spoiling the film. Mad Ron Cordry took a pigeon to the pictures under his jacket and let the poor fucking thing go during the flick. Flapping and shitting. Also he once let off a rocket in upminster Gaumont. Bouncing along the ceiling. The manager never used to walk out to do his sprout in front of the curtain in his bow tie on Sundays. Not likely. More Bangers in the ashtrays chewing gum on the velvet and dog-ends in the urinal.

Once we were all in the gaumont sitting right across sixth row being louts, when my 12 year old cousin came and said that somebody was touching him up and following him when he moved away. He sat behind us and we passed the word down the row. When my cousin shouted – He's doing it! – about 30 geezers leapt up shouting Where is he? and chased the hapless bastard's shadow down St Mary's lane as far as the park. They didn't catch him, but I bet he went to Hornchurch next week.

Dave Fryer, deft of eyebrow and wicked nuance of smirk came in the regent wearing his sunday clothing: Black etons faded lime green socks Burtons suit; fingertip drape, half-moons, reverse double-breasted lapel, single half-inch back vent, three button, middle one linked, black serge no velvet, red lining. 14″ trousers with 4″ turn-up; White boston cutaway shirt, slim jim shiny red and black diagonal striped tie, lank troubadour DA, four gold skull rings with ruby eyes, and smoking a mannikin. He'd been working for a year and was old enough for a motorbike. "I'll have you!"

"Tomorrow!"

Egg and chips two slices and a cup of tea. Ponce a fag and have a giggle. Slowly the regent began to fill up. Plenty of banter and repartee. Only a few of the real nutters would swear in front of a bird unless it was one of the girls who hung around with the team and nobody was taking their girlfriend out on a date if they were mob-handed.

"You coming down the Ritz then Dave?" "No, I'm going round Irene's for tea". Heh heh silly sod but jealous really. "Spoor's down the Mason's and his van's working. Let's have it down there you cunts." "It's a fucking long walk, I think I'll get a 370 and see you up there okay?" "Come on soldier, it ain't that far". They used to wait for me to catch up every few hundred yards and saunter on again. No fuss. Good people.

In the boozer were Noddy Miles Benny Gower, Freddy Thobald, and Paddy Tobin an ageing ted who used to say "Come and clap your laughing gear round the snotty end of my fuck-stick." He came from Dagenham cos he could be a bigger shot in peaceful little upminster maybe. When he was drunk he got flash and stroppy and thought he was top man, but mostly he was a humorous fellow. He wore a gray overcoat with a velvet collar for which he'd paid three half-crowns to somebody in a pub. Harris and Spooner were in there playing darts. Spooner was a fireman on a british railways goods engine. He was wearing his shiny sleeved waistcoat to denote it, and we used to sing "The six 5 special coming down the line with Spooner on the foot plate well overdue." Harris was a peculiarity; we'd be sitting round his house and he'd suddenly shout "Into the kitchen mother; the Kettle's got a hard on." She'd say: "You are bad to me

1980s Brian Setzer of The Stray Cats, putting on the style – as rock 'n' roll does a back-flip 25 years. Photo by Peter Anderson.

1979 Shakin' Stevens goes through the motions in the hit stageshow, *Elvis*. Photo by Anton Corbijn. Right, the inimitable original. Photo by Lloyd Dinkins.

1970S

Punk starlet Billy Idol gets back to the '50s via the '60s and lives to regret the trip. Photo by Erica Echenberg.

1950S
England's answer to Presley? Some thought that of Cliff Richard, pictured left going through the Elvis routine and wardrobe. Top right, he tries the rebel sneer, followed by an affectionate look to fellow Brit rock 'n' roller, Tommy Steele. Photos courtesy of Thames Television.

you know," and off she'd go to make the tea. We couldn't
work it out but we used to crack up laughing.

Mick the gypsy was having his usual lean and scowl. Very
flash of accoutrement including Love and Hate Knuckle
tattoos gold earring army belt donkey jacket and sideboards
that hung below his jaw. With his arm round persil which
ain't her real name. She had a small town reputation and
enjoyed it with a swagger. I bet she's still full of beans and
welcome where she goes. The youngest of the brothers
naughty could well have been there. They still run about
being naughty all over Essex. Four nice lads from the
Romford area, and if any old acquaintances read this and
say durex is bullshitting I bet they all do too. And Bobby
Goodliffe still hot from the rain-hut with love bites all round
his gregory. There were as many James Deans around then
as there were Rod Stewarts the other week.

Although some of these hounds were quite handy, the only
fightings that were likely were by way of being personal
bash-ups. Never was any territorial or sartorial codswallop a
consideration for bother. The nearest heavy teams were in
Dagenham and never went east except to the seaside. The
late teens and early 20s were subject to conscription so
maybe all the real crazies were swagged away to far-off
lands. The authorities were the only enemy but the coppers
in upminster didn't need to walk in pairs. Then as now the
young shrank very sensibly away from guidance and advice
and were glad if they got up everybody's nose. Getting
drunk and smoking gaspers was the order of the day as
regards shocking behaviour. If anybody had anything more
tasty, I wasn't put in till I had my first prel over a year later.
I didn't find out about nasal inhalers till 1959 but I was a bit
green. Divulgements concerning cuddly-ups were extremely
bad form and usually regarded as wishful thinking. If you

went to see Tammy with a young lady, nobody took the piss.

Rock'n'roll music wasn't a war-cry but a celebration. The
most rebellious stance and glower was no more than
additional elegance. There are those who suggest that
nothing has changed but I am not among them.

There was no general uprising taking place: upminster
nestled comfortably between the huge council estates of
Dagenham and Ockendon. Vandalism was pissing in the
sandpit and nicking ping-pong balls from Woolworths. It
was the time between childhood and marriage. Before
settling down occurred. There was no birth pill or legal
abortion, and if susan got pregnant on your fourth date, you
and susan got married and your haircut slowly turned into a
neglected and dying parrot as you embarked on your daily
prostrate hysterectomy lobotomy between nine and five on
weekdays and your belly got fat with boozing and you told
dirty jokes all the time which we could all see happening and
still can god help us.

For the lucky ones it was a time for being noisy and
looning about. Before nuclear scared stupid had wiped away
my radiant smile I loved rock'n'roll music for joy. Down the
windmill Hall called the Lions Den dancing to the bop was
their delight. In the regent cafe on saturday afternoons
Queenie's son used to unlock the jukebox and run his comb
across all the levers. It would still be going when she
locked up.

Doing it hard started with Lonnie. Skiffle was an instant
affair whip the mouthpiece off a phone and sing in it
through the radio Tea-chest and guitars and actual
washboard. The glass ones don't happen. Down by the
riverside by 5 o'clock Rock Island Line is a mighty good
rollock. Then Rocky prior wanted to do 20 flight Rock cos
he'd seen Eddie Cochran in the wonderful Girl Can't Help It

1977 Left, the greatest ace face of them all. Above left: even mod revivalists The Speedballs acknowledge the king. Above right: Generation X's Tony James turns the '50s image into '70s icon. Elvis photo: Rex Features. Others by Stevenson.

1980 A true fan. Photo by Peter Anderson.

Left: Leather pants and flash guitar – Eddie Cochran gives Britain a taste of the real thing in a Thames Television special, *Boys Meet Girls*. Above left: The Everly Brothers, Phil and Don, pioneer the '50s brilliantined look that became standard – even hackneyed – via a million back street barber shop pin-ups. And right: London 1980: " 'Oo you callin' acne'd, John?" Photo by Anton Corbijn. Below: Danny And The Juniors, dressed to meet that Brenda Lee dream date at the High School Hop.

1958 Buddy Holly's glasses give new hope to bespectacled wimps everywhere.

1980 The nine-stone weakling takes his ultimate revenge – in the bitter, twisted stance of Elvis Costello. The goofy grin is gone – but the NHS frames remain. Photo by Anton Corbijn.

1960 Buddy Holly looks down – as well he might – on Tommy Steele's homage delivered in a *Buddy Holly Numbers* TV show.

1981 A Freddie Garrity lookalike keeps the style alive. Photo by Graham Barker.

Motorvatin'. Saturday night cruising, the '50s teen pastime immortalised in
America Graffiti and every second song Chuck Berry ever wrote, lives on. Scenes
from San Francisco, 1980. Photos by Peter Anderson.

Jayne, Jayne, ask my agent Jayne, and I bought a drum set in aylesbury for 10/– and we called ourselves the black cats. The pop charts were closely linked with your man aldiss and brunitex and stablond barnet potions and reflected sheet music sales. Radio Luxembourg with its maddeningly wavering reception was the listening post. 6–5 special cool for cats and oh boy Dig this were on the glass. Billy Fury was the only truly magnificent rock and roller Britain produced and he wasn't discovered until much later in '59. Although primarily a balladeer he had a voice and attitude that rang in a true way. The transatlanticness of the british would be rockers made most of them sad cardboards but Billy's personality and voice steamed straight through the borrowed shapes.

So it was with little sense of angry revolt that we all climbed into the back of Terry Spoor's van. Bye bye mason's arms, Hallo road through Hornchurch to the Ritz Romford. Terry Spoor of Billiard ball crewcut horn-rims and grim countenance, emanator of sly evil asides, drove like a vicar. Sometimes 14 people got out and asked for 14 stout and milds.

There were teds there from all over the place. Canning Town Ilford Heathway Barking Southend. Hordes of them. A sea of teds. Hooting and shouting the odds and laughing. A lovely atmosphere. No policemen to be seen. The place was packed and really noisy. Disc Jockey Jamboree starring Jerry Lee Lewis Hooray and away we go. Breathless. Everybody dancing and leaping about during the numbers and singing and chanting during the bullshit plot haps. Merriments prevail until the supporting feature The Green-Eyed Blonde when footstamping and dog-end flicking commenced because of extreme boredom.

Garth, the man with the torch coming down the aisle and shouting "use the ashtrays!" and red sparks and embers bouncing off his back and leaping around his head. Great roars of laughter as somebody cuts a girls ponytail off with a flick knife: An overcoat is thrown up to the balcony and comes down in little pieces. Seats being done slice slice foam rubber chunks flying about. Crack! as the back goes. A big lump of wood sails through the air and splits the screen right through the green eyed blonde's neck. Splash! Somebody turns the fire hoses on. Then the houselights come up. Water pouring down the side aisles and policemen with dogs pouring down the middle...

It only made the Romford Recorder. Nobody got arrested. We all went and had a nice drink afterwards. My proudest moment as a subsequent rock'n'roll performer was the night the audience broke the floor of Ilford Odeon just down the road and danced on the carpet stretched over the hole. Nostalgia causes scorn these days. Scorn is fear as a frog shits in your hand.

Rock'n'roll didn't aim higher than pink cadillac and swimming pool. It fulfilled the basic human need to dress up and dance about. If Teddy Boys only had bought Bill Haley records he would never have been in the top twenty. Rebelliousness was a side-issue.

Nuclear fears and the persistent warlikeness of the yanks in Vietnam notwithstanding bunzensnines, have changed young people's awareness about their basic human requirements. The old have lived through a frightful world war and that's their hard luck. It is much harder to get hold of good cannon fodder these days. The silicone chip spreads like anthrax spores on an east wind. If the world by some quirk of nuclear impotency should survive I for one will definitely feel the urge to dress up and dance about.

"They say that rock 'n' roll will soon fade away; I know that's not true.
    Rock and roll is here to stay
    I don't want to
    *Hang up my rock 'n' roll shoes"**

Car mechanic as poet and superstar. Automobile imagery – of freedom, sex and escape – stays crucial to the modern romantic vision of Bruce Springsteen. Photo by Bob Sorce/LFI.

Above: the ring of confidence. Fats Domino, the '50s premier boogie woogie balladeer, hits on the idea for a look that will make a new man of him. Photo by Dezo Hoffman. And far right, it's 1977: yet more rings, this time worth a mint. Since wearing his haircut the wrong way round, Fats has never looked back. Photo by Anton Corbijn. Right: rockin' at London's Southgate Royalty, 1980. Brylcreem Ltd claims three more satisfied customers. Photos by Anton Corbijn.

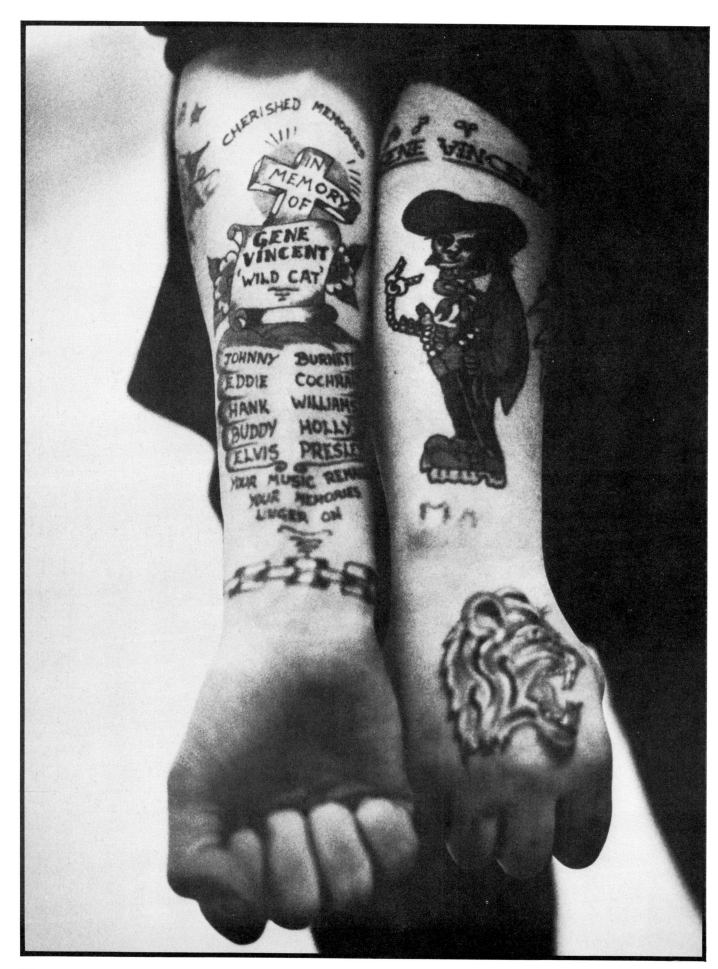

Left: in memoriam, a tattoo'd graveyard for the rock 'n' roll stars. Photo taken in early 1980 by Anton Corbijn. Top: one of those 'fearsome' stars, Gene Vincent, terrorises the chorus line. Photo courtesy of Thames Television. Above right: Vincent in his celebrated leathers. Photo: Rex Features. Above left: modern rocker with the bottle to be an '80s wild cat. Photo by Peter Anderson.

Below: 1981 rock 'n' roll purists, as always, dressed up. Quiffs, sideburns, drapes and drainpipe trousers compulsory. And for the boys . . . Photos by Graham Barker.

Right: Little Richard hits swinging London and poses in front of Gaylord's. For one of the most renowned glam rock 'n' rollers, he is dressed down in casual 'tourist' wear. Photo by Dezo Hoffman.

Right: "Was he looking for dress tips? At any rate, 17 year old Edwardian-dressed John Barre of Glasgow was at St Enoch station to greet these French mannequins. And the girls – well wrapped up for the cold weather – seemed just as interested in John's garb as he was in theirs." January 1957, and the media struggles to come to terms with it all. Photo by Paul Popper.

28

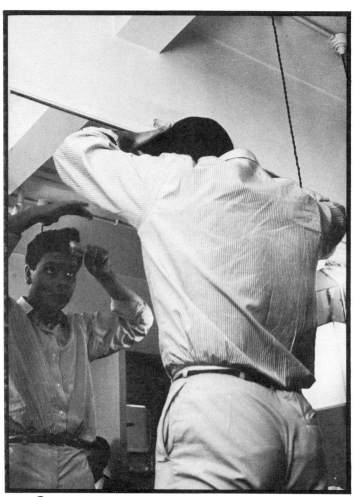

1960 No respectable rock 'n' roller ever said goodbye to '50s style. Cliff Richard gets his quiff in shape. Photo by Dezo Hoffman.

1980 In front of his Elvis altar, the Ted remembers '50s narcissism and runs the rake through the grease. Photo by Peter Anderson.

1980 And the rockabilly kid shows that there are more important things to do in the toilet than pee. Photo by Anton Corbijn.

The Small Faces   Photo by David Wedgbury/Decca Records

The Sixties
THE TOTAL LOOK
By Paul Weller

In general you can't put a value on style because it's so personal. Perhaps that's its appeal. It's like a million people telling me that Picasso was a genius; well, I think he was shite and that a French Small Faces EP cover can piss all over any of his paintings. So, to understand my involvement with the '60s, you have to realise that it's made up from this 'style', and that it can't be viewed or judged alongside anything else. Its influence on me is total, but not blinding.

My interest is with the style years – the Total Look – from 1963 to 1967. It covers a whole range, from the early Mod(ernists) to swinging young dandies and up until the hedonistic hippies. It's a purely aesthetic and quite possibly superficial interest; very rarely does it extend past clothes, music, films and books. Politicians are politicians, they're all the same eternal scum as far as I'm concerned. So I've no interest in '60s economics or politics; save for, perhaps, the student riots of 1968 when it seemed the whole (young) world caught fire. Their intentions and radicalism are laudable, but I can't help feeling it was another luxury in the hands of the middle classes.

It's also these once young radicals that have clogged up a lot of channels for today's working class youth. I suppose I'm talking primarily about music, TV and the media in general; but it has been these old bastards who won't get out of the way for the new generations, and this has caused a bottleneck. Anyway, I don't mean to knock them too much; I doubt if I would have the bottle to shove a flower down a gun barrel, if bottle is indeed the quality in question.

I first became interested in the early '60s Mods in late 1974. I can't properly remember how or why. I think it was possibly through seeing a photograph of a group, and I also remember a couple of letters in the *New Musical Express* from some original Mods who described their lifestyle at the time. In any case it interested me deeply and I tried to find out more about it. The most important aspect was the music of the '70s: I hated all of it, until the glorious, liberating Sex Pistols in 1976! Before them it was all the clutching-at-straws glam bollocks; all the soft nonsense, Philly 'soul', and the terrible MOR stuff. Bowie and Bolan were okay, but I even lost interest in them after their third or fourth LPs.

Instead, I went back and listened to the early R&B, R&R and soul records, and The Beatles who I had always been a fan of anyway. I think it was the stylelessness and bland facelessness of the '70s that induced my '60s obsessions. There was nothing to be part of, you know, nothing to base myself on (and I am talking pre-punk remember).

At the time we – The Jam – were still playing Chuck Berry songs and the obligatory R&R standards with which we were rapidly becoming bored. I saw that through becoming a Mod it would give me a base and an angle to write from, and thus the group would take on an individual identity. And this we eventually did. We went out and bought black suits and started playing Motown, Stax and Atlantic covers. I bought a Rickenbacker guitar, a Lambretta GP 150 and tried to style my hair like Steve Marriott's circa '66. I felt so individual and arrogant because of it. It was like my own little esoteric world, people stared and thought I looked strange.

It was exactly the same effect The Sex Pistols had on me and my mates after we saw them in '76. Oh, the blasé arrogance the day after in the local pub!

"You've never seen them?"

"You've never heard of The Sex Pistols or Johnny Rotten?!"

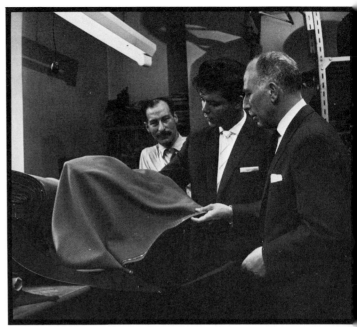

They were *ours*, our own private little group which all the
uncool people had never heard of! Well, that's the same
feeling I had about the Mods. Most kids my age had never
heard of Mods, or, at the most, could barely remember them.
Like some mythical beast from the Dark Ages. My own
crusade!

If it's facts or chronological fashion changes you want, you
need only look at the photos. They say everything about the
'60s: one picture of Steve Marriott or a 19 year old Pete
Townshend says it all! Well, these pictures spoke to me (they
still do actually), and I conjured up my own image of what
the Mods were about. I saw them as clean, smart, working
class, arrogant, anti-authoritarian with absolutely no respect
for their elders.

The whole image is C-O-O-L: dancing into the small
hours, blocked, finger clickin' to J.B. and the Famous
Flames, even smokin' to Bluebeat! Shopping on Saturday
morning in Carnaby Street or watching Pete Townshend
smash all that 'valuable' equipment. It's this imagery that
appeals to me. It's also this very same imagery that made the

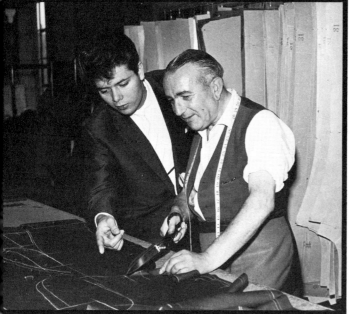

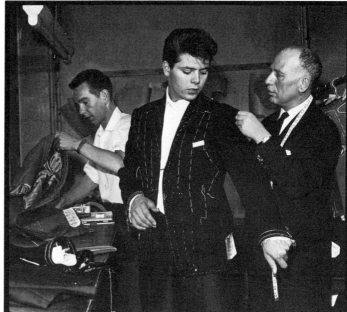

"Britain's No.1 young entertainer, Cliff Richard, leaves for America today. Whilst there he will appear on American TV and tour with the 'Biggest Stars Of 1960'. Yesterday, in between rehearsals for the Sunday Night at the London Palladium show, Cliff was being fitted by London tailor, Lew Rose, for his suits for the tour. This Spring, checks are bang in fashion, and so Cliff has included a smart Lovat Glen check in his wardrobe." Photos by Dezo Hoffman. Didn't he do well?

1979 Mod revival seem like an anachronism.

Prats like Ian Page, a once failed Punk Star who then tried his hand at Mod, told the lads that punk was dead and had never lived up to its promises anyway, and the only way to win in the rat race was by joining the bastards in their own game! What? It was the complete antithesis of the original '60s Mod movement. *They* didn't want to join in anyone's fucking game, they played their own and made their own rules; if you didn't like it you could f-f-f-fade away!

The '79 revival was also a little saddening and cheapening for the kids involved, it just seemed so desperate, these young working class kids trying their best to dress up and look the part while all around their environment was crumbling. So, perhaps they did get that part right: after all, was it not Mod mentor and The Who's first manager, Pete Meadon who described Mod as "clean living under difficult circumstances"?

People are always telling me about the disparity between Mod and Punk, but it's something I could never (and still can't) see. The Modernists created their own scene just as

Punk did (albeit with an entrepreneurial helping hand from Malcolm McLaren). Both movements came from the kids themselves and relied on no one else for support (Mod particularly, I think). They created their own clubs, music, lifestyles and clothes shops.

In fact, the first time I went to the 100 Club in London's Oxford Street, it seemed as if I was walking onto a '60s film set. Troggs and Kinks records were blaring up the stairs; The Clash clanged out their tinny Kinks-derivative riffs. Short hair! Individual looking kids! The Pistols' noisy garage band racket and Rotten's youthful amphetamined arrogance. I loved it! It was so YOUNG and EXCITING, and of course, there were NO FLARES – one of the most hideous fashion creations ever!

It's fantastic when kids create their own scenes, but as with anything once its popularity spreads and, more importantly, the media get hold of it, that's it! You might as well kiss it goodbye. The media have killed so much young spirit with their crass commercialism that it's sickening. They did the same with the original Mod movement – throwing together

1961 Above: Adam Faith: sartorial perfectionist, right down to the cut of his pyjamas. Right: An amazing quick-change act – two new outfits modelled without moving a single inch. Photos by Dezo Hoffman.

1960

Above: "Tommy Steele will not be in topper and tails for his wedding tomorrow to showgirl Ann Donoghue. He has chosen a cool suit in navy blue silk instead, which has cost him £45 and weighs eight ounces a yard. Tommy, standing in his stocking feet, admires his new suit when he tried it on at his Piccadilly tailors yesterday." Photo Keystone.

1963 Above: Mersey boomers The Fourmost line up in classic beat group style for Dezo Hoffman, the photographer largely responsible for British beat's image in the first half of the '6os. Photo courtesy of EMI Records (UK).

1977 Dezo's influence is felt in this publicity pic of The Jam. Notice their choice of two-tone shoes. This footwear was to become known simply as "Jam shoes". Photo courtesy of Polydor Records.

1963 Rock is fun and smartness as Britain goes beat crazy, later followed by America: winklepickers and carefully rehearsed Liverpool accents. Above: John McNally of The Searchers. Photo by Dezo Hoffman. Top: John Lennon, in Pierre Cardin Beatle togs, has meaningful encounter with Helen Shapiro: Photo: Matthews' News And Photo Agency. Below right: The Beatles and The Rolling Stones define the time in black and white. Clean shirts and short hair, rock 'n' roll innocents all. Ha! Photos by Dezo Hoffman.

1980 Chas and Suggs of Madness go formal for Associated Television's *Tiswas* show. Photo by Anton Corbijn.

1963 The Beatles, appearing on BBC TV's *Morecombe And Wise Show*, offer a few useful tips. Photo by Dezo Hoffman.

Sunday supplements on the club scene and so attracting the bright young things from Chelsea (well, who else reads the Sunday supplements?).

I saw the very same thing happen to Punk, especially at the Roxy Club in Covent Garden. All those ageing, middle class wankers in their £30 bondage trousers. Oh, how outrageous darling, showing a glimpse of freshly washed nipple. And *whaaat?* Two girls kissing!

The other side of the media, the prole papers, attracted the other Mod, the moron element, certain to eliminate any promising young scene. It was this lot who started the boring Mod versus Rockers seaside riots in the '60s. It was nothing at all to do with the real Modernists and stylists who wouldn't have anything to do with anything so crass and

1965 Left: The Who, lined up for an early Decca publicity shot, matched mod fashion with '60s pop art. The impact of Pete Townshend's union jack jacket lingers on. Photo by David Wedgbury/Decca Records. And right, another Wedgbury photo for the 'My Generation' sleeve.

1977 Below left: The Jam remember mod and Pete's jacket. Photo by Elaine Bryant/LFI.

1979 Below right: New York new wavers Blondie remember the LP sleeve too. The target T-shirt was another key symbol of mod style. Photo by Joe Stevens.

vulgar, and quite rightly they turned their backs on the new moronic Mod interlopers . . . "It was as though we were taking over the country."

Yes, mate, that's just what 'they' wanted you to think. Where are you now, in nick or raving with the wife? That's not a criticism on my part; it's a game the establishment always plays with youth: it goes on for a while, they let you think you're winning, but they turn the tables at the last moment – or is it that we just get bored?

Perhaps the last real surviving link with the original Mods is the wonderful Northern Soul Scene. A couple of my mates were into Northern Soul and I remember them taking me to an all-nighter. These lads ain't there to pose or fight, they have one purpose – to dance and enjoy themselves.

1966 Above left: The Kinks, dedicated followers of fashion, in the latest fab gear. Ray Davies takes a peek over his pilot shades, while brother Dave looks particularly pleased with his tartan bell-bottom hipsters. Above right: the Carnaby Street army marches on as The Jam (for it is they, yet again) go walkabout in the London fashion street where it all started.

1964 Right: Rod 'The Mod' Stewart, his hair combed to perfection – before some vulture landed there six years later and made a nest out of it. Photo by David Wedgbury/Decca Records.

1966 The Small Faces' Steve Marriott demonstrating the fine art of centre-parting. Photo by Napier Russell.

1981 The Jam's Paul Weller looking back at an acknowledged major influence. Paul bears more than a passing resemblance to Steve in this photo by Anton Corbijn.

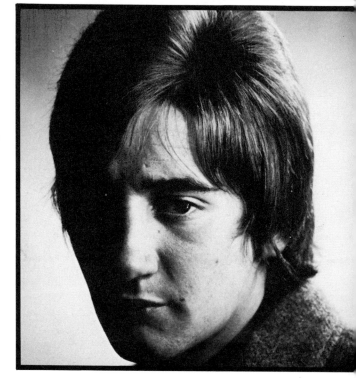

1965/66
46

Left to right: three young hopefuls – Marc Bolan 1965, David Bowie and Cat Stevens in 1966. All photos by David Wedgbury/Decca Records.

Hedonists maybe, but with a real dedication. They still play a lot of the early Mod soul sounds and obscure soul stuff. The clothes are quite different, but you're nearly always bound to see a few beautifully decorated scooters outside. Long may you spin, jump and back-flip and finish off with Deanne Parrish!

By 1965 the real Mod movement was dying except in a few provincial towns and up North. As for London, where it all started after all, it had been taken over by the young jet set. Britain was now moving into its Swinging Sixties period.

A few batches of Mods battled on bravely, just like zombies silently marching towards their Mecca (ballroom) in the shape of Brighton or Margate every Bank Holiday. It makes me think of a song I never got round to finishing called, 'The Last Of The Scooter Boys'. Sad, eh?

While the scene became diluted and commercial, taken over by entrepreneurs and such like, I still think the '65/'66 period produced some of the best music ever and some of the greatest clothes styles. Mod had had a vast effect on the bands, who'd actually copied the kids' way of dress rather than vice versa. Where would The Who be now if they had never been in contact with Mod? Townshend has always gone to great lengths to explain the influence Mod had on him. Small Faces, Rod Stewart, David Bowie and Marc Bolan – all of them came out of the Mod scene.

But by 1965 big business had taken the reins again and were peddling fashions *back* to the kids, while the bands were becoming more and more outrageous, using contrived styles of clothes only as gimmicks. The Who adopted their questionable pop-art clobber (and music!); The Creation, who copied them, took their action art canvases on stage. Even more so in 1966, there were bands like The Move from Birmingham projecting a gangster look; The New Vaudeville Band chose a 1920s look and sound. And what are we still seeing today? Every band on the BBC's weekly TV show *Top Of The Pops* have got themselves a Total Image: Stray Cats, Spandau Ballet, Adam And The Ants; except none of it is new, it's been done and done and done, time and time again.

After all, what is revivalism? For me it's just another word for people clutching at straws, looking for another opening to squeeze through. And the same can be said of the '65/'66 period with its fashions and clothes.

Whereas the Mods were original, the Swinging Sixties era was a hotchpotch of styles – the old, if-you-throw-enough-shit-at-the-wall-some-of-it-has-gotta-stick syndrome. Mind you, that might be a bit of an over-reaction on my part; perhaps it was just this (comparatively) affluent generation looking for laughs. Whatever, this particular period heralded Britain as the centre of youth culture, ornamented with Union Jack clocks, socks, trays and shirts. "I'm backing Britain," the badges read, without the least hint of jingoism (see, patriotism can be fun!). It was all done with a sense of frivolity, almost as if Harold Wilson himself (for it was he) not only approved of the young's actions but wholeheartedly encouraged it, what with the Fab Four getting MBEs and all.

But I'm still not sure whether this picture of the '60s is the real one or the one I've been conditioned into imagining with too many re-runs of the 1966 movie, *Blow up*. But the badges and MBEs definitely existed.

The real and positive side of this period was that the young were given more control in certain areas, like the theatre, films, music, literature. And although this might be hard to swallow, young DJs also became a major influence on British radio for the first time. When pirate ships were outlawed in 1967, the government was forced to create the first official youth oriented radio station, Radio One, and employ many of the former pirate DJs.

George Melly wrote in great detail about the late '50s and early '60s in his retrospective, *Revolt Into Style* (Penguin). It's

1966 A clothes shop in Carnaby Street swinging to the sounds of pop music and cash registers. Photo by Dezo Hoffman.

1966 In the street outside before it was made a pedestrian precinct, a mod in parka with his most prized possession between his legs. Photo: Rex Features.

1981 Welling mod and his scooter, learning to do it all over again, right down to the parka and authentic desert boots. Photo by Muriel Roe.

1965 The Small Faces pave the wave, even if this David Wedgbury photo is reminiscent of the 'My Generation' sleeve.

1979 Mod revivalists The Fixations pose on the beach, that hallowed Bank Holiday battleground. Photo by Stevenson.

1979 More modern mods, on London's Tower Bridge, see the past flash before their eyes. Photo by Mike Laye.

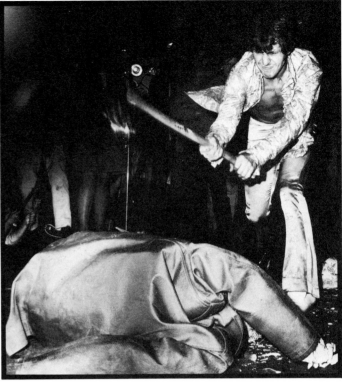

ANARCHY IN THE UK

"They're smashing," ran the caption to these action shots of The Move from the mid-'60s, whipping up excitement (and just a little publicity) by applying the cut-up technique to Adolf Hitler, an effigy of Prime Minster Harold Wilson and, finally, their own equipment. Keen amateur axeman Bev Bevan (top right) went on to become a respectable member of society as the staunchly Tory drummer of ELO. Photos by Bobby Davidson.

Opposite: Sex Pistol Johnny Rotten carried on the time-honoured shock/horror/outrage tradition with his group's devastatingly obscene appearance on a British TV tea-time news show. "The Filth And The Fury!" screamed next day's papers in December, 1976. Photo Stevenson.

worth getting hold of if you want to know more about the Swinging London club scene, though like another '60s youth culture book, *Generation X*, it's far too clinical and obviously written by an 'outsider' to be that accurate. But the significance of these books was that for the first time people were actually taking young people seriously and desperately trying to analyse them.

By 1966, having had a couple of years to assimilate the British musical invasion – spearheaded by The Beatles and followed by a whole bunch of marketable commodities when the Fab Britain Fever gripped the States – America exported its own groups and scene back to the UK. Along with The Byrds, Grateful Dead, Mothers Of Invention, Jefferson Airplane and the rest, came acid, mysticism, free-thinking and bohemianism. Peace and love were (and still are) admirable sentiments . . . but if they have to be induced by drugs, what's the fucking point?

Compared to the so-called British underground groups, the Americans were crap. It was just blues speeded up, extended with tedious guitar soloing with a few, "Far outs!" in between. Howlin' Wolf with headbands!

In any case, the centre of the new youth culture switched from Britain and London's Carnaby Street to America and San Francisco's Haight-Ashbury area – which is still there, full of clapped-out, filthy degenerates, still saying peace and love man, then asking you to show how much you love them by donating a couple of bucks for their junk habits.

The advent of the hippies' scene, which had been growing underground since 1965, tended to polarise fashion and musical styles; it seemed there was either pop or there was 'serious' music. In their day the Mods had shown the same kind of elitism and hate of commerciality, but perhaps not quite as dogmatically as those in the underground who even turned their backs on soul music!

51

1967 The psychedelic explosion found its ultimate expression in the music – and style – of Jimi Hendrix. In 'All Along The Watchtower' he took the lyrics of Bob Dylan and created a wild acid vision of his own. Photo by Dezo Hoffman.

1977 Left: Dylan's own 'Blonde On Blonde' back pages have been lovingly re-created in the look of John Cooper Clarke, the punk poet, the 'back-combed Bard of Salford'. Photo by Kevin Cummins. And below left, the young Dylan offers another evocative icon in the repertoire of Generation X's Tony James. Photo by Stevenson.

1965 Above: "Lissen, if youse limeys rip me off just one more time . . ." Photo by Dezo Hoffman.

Another similarity was that the media again grabbed their chance of yet more sensationalism at the expense of the hippies with lurid descriptions of their sex, fashion and lifestyles, thus attracting more sharks ready with their instant kaftans, love beads and joss sticks. 1967 was the summer of love, and *all* that entailed.

The nucleus of the British underground movement was mainly organised by the art college mob and the middle class quasi-activists, with new bands like The Pink Floyd, Soft Machine, the Jimi Hendrix Experience and Cream. Hendrix inspired and gave fashion credibility to the Afro hairstyle (and will he ever be forgiven?). Weirdness found an identity with the Floyd's mentor and original guitarist, singer and writer, the brilliant Syd Barrett, as much a bizarre dresser as personality.

Another group whose records symbolise the flippancy and superficiality of the hippie period were John's Children, at one time featuring Marc Bolan. Their records were all about flowers, young girls and sex; all very Beardsley and decadent-evil. And I always see the style of 1967 along the same lines as the 1920s – the affluent, hedonistic society, going at such a fast pace. In fact, all of the '60s seem to have been lived at a furious speed, with styles, attitudes and music all changing so rapidly.

So here ends my interest. As someone once said to me, you need only look at the pictures of The Beatles from '63 to '69 to note all the changes. In '63 they were fresh faced, optimistic youths; in '67 they were expanding their minds, young men in search of knowledge; by the end of the decade they were hardened, disillusioned old men.

I feel no pity nor respect really; you pay your money, you take your choice. But now it seems that the attitudes towards young people are regressing to those pre-'56: they're being swept back under the rug.

In reality the rug never went away in the '60s, they just took it to the cleaners for a while.

1967 When Haight turned to love – hippies freak out San Francisco, before growing up and going home. Photo: Rex Features.

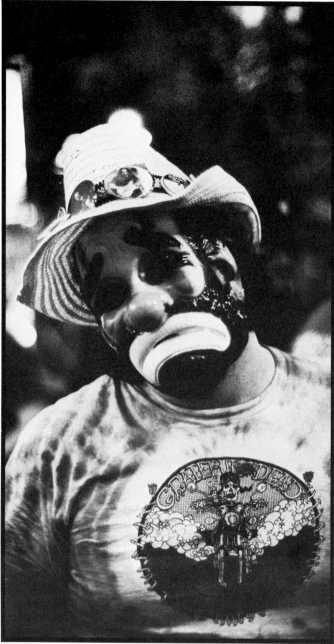

1980 In San Francisco 13 years later, a Dead head wonders what he's got to be grateful for. Photo by Peter Anderson.

1967 Fab Four grow old, grow weird, grow moustaches. In that order. Photo by Dezo Hoffman.

1980 Texan hippie fails to twig it's all over. Photo by Peter Anderson.

1967 Above: Mason, Wood and Winwood – collectively Traffic – lay down a soundtrack to the Summer of Love. Below: lovebeads, blissed-out smiles and mystic Eastern chic – The Move do their best, but credibility eludes them. Roy Wood (seated), in Sergeant Pepper surplus, keeps one eye open for the next bandwagon.

1969   Looking more angelic than any choirboy, Pete Townshend of The Who. But that guitar had only seconds to live. Photo by Stevenson.

1969   After flower power the hippies turned to a new hard rock underground. Doors singer Jim Morrison was one of its prophets. Photo by Barry Plummer.

1969 Family's Roger Chapman – technicolour whimsy gave way to unrepentant scruffiness. Headbands went out, headbangers came in. Photo by Robert Ellis.

Viv Albertine of The Slits. Photo by Anton Corbijn.

Girlstyle
WORN OUT: CAREER CHIC
By Cynthia Rose

'It's easy to join but who establishes it?''
Diana Vreeland, *Chatting About Style*

Rock music has evolved into the Western world's foremost live attraction and one of its most well-publicised commodities. Originally its myths and iconographies were plundered from those of Hollywood and popular mass culture, but along the way it has both reacted to and made use of mainstream notions about glamour, sexuality, wealth, celebrity, and – since the '60s – hipnitude. Through the images offered up by its performers and its presenters (the promoters, packagers and advertisers), the public has developed a corpus of ideas about what rock style and rock fashion are – and what they stand for.

Often these attitudes have had social effects and consequences; always they have had social reflections. For, next to the music itself, it is the rock performer's dress, the appearance of a personal style, through which the audience most directly associates the artist with particular characteristics and attitudes. And the themes of rock style are inseparable from the thematic concerns of rock itself: sex, violence, images of the feminine and masculine, references to other media such as film, literature and the visual arts, and evocations of luxury or poverty.

Popular concepts about leisure, indulgence and play are also altered or embodied in rock as an entertainment form – and in any sartorial trappings rock may affect. Rock style has never been some sort of folk art which arose from the awkward vitalities of the folk (however *they* might be defined). Nor is it something which continues to rise, cyclical and phoenix-like, from some collective gene-pool of intuitions, sensibilities and indigenous propensities.

No, rock style is a complex little aesthetic-nostalgic-mercantile miracle which derives itself over and over again from two prototypes. One is that mainstream idea of glamour which hails from the canons of showbiz and depends on a theatricality directly influenced by the stage, the screen and popular ideas of their style of stardom.

The other determinant can be topicality – the god of retail designers and marketing men worshipped more obliquely and independently as 'the cool' or 'the hip'. The search for style which comes under the influence of these dictates is likely to be more individual and will often move from the particular to the general, looking for some identity that will be separate from (and stronger than) the mainstream of identities which surrounds it. The identity of rock's 'hip' dresser often specifically addresses or reflects contemporary events, issues and conflicts.

What is the relationship of music's female performers to rock style? Historically, rock music has simply failed to take on woman except as an idol or target. On these terms she remains indispensable to the actual making of the music, with its assertions of male supremacy and its Erotic Agony upholstering. Yet society has offered the women of rock something even less stable: much worship with little esteem. Generally, her work has been regarded as a sophisticated hobby or a simple pursuit of status. And, traditionally, her *real* art has been publicity – playing the game by its own rules through choosing her image from among the already available fantasies . . . and then maybe undercutting it with a little irony.

Performance adornment has always been one of the few angles of image over which the female rock performer has hope of wielding any real control; hence its personal importance to the artist herself, when all around her marketers and big money consort on how best to fix her features in the mind of the consumer. Women serious about

their rock inherit two careers – their music is one, and transcending the age-old marketing images they will be expected to vindicate is another.

To understand just how entrenched these images are, one must look back to the '50s, the era of high school with all its year books inscribed "Stay as sweet as you are". The '50s began with the popular music business under the control of a few middle-aged businessmen who were making money with things as they were. They had a formulaic approach to both the production and presentation of pop – and their ideas of change were confined to a novelty gimmick here or there.

Like the music, the clothes worn by performers were dictated by adults and shaped according to generally accepted notions of propriety and occasion. That '50s music (both black and white) which was mainstream pop was first and foremost goodtime music, and the dress of the women who contributed to it reflected their socially inculcated ideas about dressing to Go Out, to hit the town. The reigning black music was straighter about sex and cloaked it less in euphemistic rainbows and roses – male R&B artists or balladeers like Wynonie Harris, Chuck Berry, Bo Diddley, and Jackie Wilson dressed like the slick, no-good seducers their music often portrayed, in flash and racy versions of sharp '50s styles as streamlined as the cars in Chuck Berry's lyrics and as smooth as Dixie Peach pomade. Their female counterparts like Laverne Baker and Ruth Brown dressed to attract as well – the sexual come-on of their clothes was more direct and less socially constricted than that of their white female counterparts (such as Connie Francis and Helen Shapiro), who aimed to convey femininity as well as the female.

The difference was mirrored in the music: definite targets and calculations lay behind the romanticising and daydreaming of white vocalists (finding the one true boyfriend destined to become husband, provider and father; aiming straight for the common and accepted ideal of home, kids and possessions). Seen in terms of their blues-based preoccupations, the attitude of the black women singers was defiant; the content of their songs (evolving as it did within a social fabric of discrimination, poverty and blunted hopes) was franker about sexual infidelity, the fleeting nature of pleasure, and the basic hardships of day-to-day living. Sexual choice (and especially the theatrically isolated image of the singer dressed to kill – the visualisation of a single night's determined hedonism) was one of few avenues of personal rebellion against the dreary conventions of the era.

These assumptions helped contribute the visual and psychological background to the phenomenon of the teenager, which burst upon the public in the '50s. An early indication of the coming upheaval was an outbreak of juvenile delinquency: hoods in the States and Teds in Britain. Both tribes developed rigid codes of dress but lacked other areas in which to channel their newfound togetherness and restless isolation. The force which soon claimed these rebellious energies was rock and roll.

When businessmen realised that there was a commercial goldmine in the new teen community, fashion was one of the first areas they annexed. The rituals of the girlish bedroom, the rites of girl culture – like motorbikes, hair curlers, make-up and mohair were quickly labelled teen by marketing men with sales in mind. The new sound may have been a fusion of the rebellious black music of the era with the white ballad tradition, but commercially it became and remained a mostly white, mostly middle and lower middle class phenomenon. Its lyrics supplied the first myths (high school, the million-dollar teardrops of Teen Romance, and the morbid death songs of thwarted Teen Passion) which were not adult hand-me-downs. And its singers (used, abused and shaped though they were by adult management) became the first rock idols and heroines – adored through imitation.

1958 The cool Elvis prefers to watch the dance floor rather than this lady's somewhat bizarre creation. Photo by Lloyd Dinkins.

1980 Boy and girl get much closer outside a South London Rock 'n' Roll Skirts And Petticoat shop. Photo by Peter Anderson.

1980 Teddy girl models satin dress and pointed shoes, pure '50s style. Photo by Peter Anderson.

1980 And beneath the skirt are the layers of petticoats. Elvis gets back in the picture. Photo by Peter Anderson.

1960s

Real cool girlstyle imported into Britain by the Americans. Left: Innez Fox poses in her stage dress, just getting the edge on spivvy Charlie. Photo by Dezo Hoffman. Top left: Diana Ross pioneers the turban hairstyle while with The Supremes. Photo courtesy of Thames Television. Above: The Ronettes look streetwise and funky. Photo by David Wedgbury/Decca Records. And top right: Patti Smith exhibits her idols, a T-shirt, military trousers and ballet shoes. Confused? So was photographer Kate Simon.

1964

Pop singer Lulu as innocent, aspiring fashion model (weren't they all?). This photograph by David Wedgbury /Decca Records shows the Scots star who condemns sex before marriage in a fetching but sensible trouser suit. Unfortunately they ran out of material before completing the sleeves and legs.

Performance fashions in the '50s filtered out to the suburbs through album covers, public appearances, TV, movie roles and fan magazines – evolving from year book poses and dress to the individualised styles of the emerging stars: Annette Funicello, Ruby Murray, Sandra Dee, Connie Stevens, Shelley Fabares, Brenda Lee and Connie Francis. But the female singer was always cast as the representative of popularity and sweetness, those teen gods of the '50s – Annette could aspire to nothing higher than her status as dream date for Frankie Avalon, just as the emerging Girl Groups sang of an aching passion and longing for the One Boy.

The '50s teen idolette was defined by the preferences of her male counterpart (it's easy to imagine The Four Freshmen or The Mellokings dating The Originals or The Angels) and they wore exactly what *your* dream date would like you to wear, if you earned all the money they did. The pairings of teenage stars in the movies and on TV (Frankie Avalon and Annette; Ed 'Kookie' Byrnes and Connie Stevens in *77 Sunset Strip*; and Shelley Fabares and Paul Petersen on *The Donna Reed Show*) heavily promoted these ideas of female stars' dress as pure dating adornment; an embellishment of the *status quo* more than an embellishment of the individual woman.

The women of the '50s who really undercut this mainstream orientation were the Cheap Girls: The Shangri-Las, The Ronettes and The Ikettes (and later, those troupes of TV show dancers such as the Gazzari Dancers and *Shindig*'s go-go team). The Shangri-Las were always nice girls mourning the traumas of falling in love with a social misfit – but it was clear their Beatnik-mode clothes could have contributed to the fact that they constantly found themselves in messy situations . . . they wore trousers, for one thing (often black) as well as leathers, plastic, and boots. The Ronettes dressed more 'feminine' (because they weren't white?) and the overpowering sexuality of their wasp waists, stiletto heels and cascading wigs was as pervasive and obvious as a cheap perfume.

The Cheap Girl singers gave teenhood a continuous shot of *West Side Story*-style romance: ever-poignant and ever-doomed (for in the '50s to oppose the *status quo* pre-ordained disaster). Yet as much as they represented the perils of playing with social ostracism, they embodied also the undeniable lure of the back seat, the steamy night and the

MARY QUANT NO-NONSENSE MAKE-UP

More scenes of '60s innocent glamour. Top left: Dusty Springfield, old black eyes, shows the practicality of eye make-up three inches deep. Photo: SKR. Centre: She demonstrates the smart evening gown look of '60s pop. Photo courtesy of Thames Television. Top right: Little Brenda Lee projects the girl-next-door-image who just *happens* to be plugging her latest record for the camera of David Wedgbury/Decca Records. Above: The person who introduced the mini-skirt in 1965 now advertises "No-nonsense make-up". Something of a contradiction in terms, no doubt.

sexual quest. And so they have endured in ways their sisters with the charm-school manners have not – the echoes of the Cheap Girl singers and their style can be detected in the musics of Bette Midler, Patti Smith and Bruce Springsteen (where they appear also as characters). Their longings were rock's archetypal Young Lust; their 'look' was symbolic of rock's recurrent rebellion and theatrical sass.

By the early '6os more serious concerns had superseded the suburban teenage ideal – the civil rights campaigns and peace movement were beginning to appeal to the hearts and imaginations of youth via the renaissance of folk and ballad musics with the heightened political and Romantic concerns. Those who copied the casual, bohemian attire identified with the folkies were often labelled Beatniks, and their sombre fashions and plain hairstyles were taken to indicate humourlessness as much as seriousness. But the charisma of the folkies increased with the popularity of singer/ songwriters like Judy Collins, Joan Baez, Mary Travers and Joni Mitchell. These new stars with their exotic, often gypsy-like attire redolent of odd hours, restless travel and romantic quests, symbolised an alternative path for their audiences which led eventually to the colourful hippie heyday.

Star women folk singers did not really differentiate their performance clothing from anything else they wore, and emulation of their styles became for the first time a tacit indication of an imitator's alternative opinions about life and politics. But by 1964 the reigning folk forms, with their romanticism and promises, sounded a bit too much like the echoes of false prophecy – too tied to the recently broken dreams of America's New Frontier. And ready to fill the gap this left was a music of patent exuberance, emanating from Britain – raucous but innocuous and not a bit hip . . . *yet*. It was evolving from the youth underground of foppish Mods and leather-loving, Ted-type Rockers. And the fashion demarcations between the Mods and Rockers were second only in importance to that music which claimed their allegiance – one fuelled the other directly.

The Swinging Sixties and the British takeover of rock were even more important as an event and a mood than they were as music, for the image-consciousness and consumer fever they engendered were truly phenomenal. This was the point in time when the rock personality began to exert a powerfully direct influence on style, retail designs, and marketing – as well as on social concepts of sex relations and romance.

In the beginning, the British sound was still clean-cut, tidy and generally well behaved – purveyed by a series of singing fashion indices like Kathy Kirby, Cilla Black, Lulu and Sandie Shaw; the girls-next-door-made-good. Dusty Springfield added some guts, and Queen Of The Mods Cathy McGowan led and shaped style as a television presenter . . . the first such non-singing personality to exert fashion influence as a friend of the stars. It was the point at which The Rolling Stones (eventually to become the popular imagination's personification of the ultimate rock group with the ultimate rock style) had yet to dress too differently from their fellows – they were just scruffier and neglected to adopt the Mod legacy of neat suits and ties. Their real metamorphosis was to take place later under the influence of psychedelia and revolutionary airs.

Fashion began to merge with the hot commodity of the new music largely through social channels. Models like Penelope Tree and Patti Boyd, actresses from Jane Asher to the underground stars like Edie Sedgwick and Ultra Violet, designers ljke Angela Cash and Betsey Johnson, socialites from Baby Jane Holzer to the Ormsby-Gore sisters, started to hang around with and date male rock personalities. And their photographer cohorts recorded it all, which fanned the publicity. More than the real girl singers, Twiggy and Jean Shrimpton emerged as the female faces of the new sound. Because it was now rock's hostesses – the girlfriends of the

"At Cathy McGowan's request, Lee Cooper have man tailored – for beach and pleasure – white toweling Hip-trousers. Cathy will be wearing these and other Lee Cooper clothes on Rediffusion's *Ready, Steady, Go!* programme February 12th onwards. Available throughout the country. Retail price 32/6d. Colours: True White. Material: 100% cotton."

TALKING HEAD AS SALES MODEL

"Yes, it's going to be a corduroy Hip-Trouser year for girls. *Ready, Steady, Go!* interviewer Cathy McGowan has designs in super bold corduroy – colours Oyster and Cool Black. Man tailored by Mr. Lee Cooper – Fly fronts, hug hips, flares out at ankle. Retails at 47/6d."

"*Ready, Steady, Go!* girl Cathy McGowan now tries her hand at designing with Lee Cooper, Europe's leading jean manufacturers. She chooses Hip-Skirts in bold corduroy with bold ½″ full length brass zips – topped with the large brass ring. Retail price: 45/–."

The Queen of Mod sells out.

1967 "On Thursday (28-9-67) at Goringes in Victoria, London, a new 'Go Go Boutique' opened featuring a special range of 'Sandie Shaw' fashions. Sandie, herself, visited the store on Thursday. All the Goringes assistants wear 'Sandie Shaw' dresses."

1968 "Of all people, Sandie Shaw the singer, who always sings barefoot, is marketing SANDIE SHAW SHOES. On Wednesday (28-8-68) Sandie presented her first Shoe Collection . . . Sandie herself wore a white wig and was wearing some Isadora Duncan-style shoes which are retailed at 99/11d."

Photos: Syndication International.

stars – who did more than merely reflect the prevailing fab off-the-peg styles. As stars in their own right, they drew attention to the whole group of younger name designers they patronised: Mary Quant, Ossie Clark, Mr Freedom, Angela Cash, Betsey Johnson, Paraphenalia, and the Kings Road, Carnaby Street and New York City boutiques which showcased their wares. They also associated these designers explicitly with the newness and hipness *of* rock.

This was an important change in focus – the status of figures like Marianne Faithfull, Jane Ormsby-Gore and Twiggy as fashion-setters in the pop sphere was to continue through similar figures right up to the ascendancy of strong women rock *stars* like Grace Slick and Janis Joplin. Jean and Chrissie Shrimpton, Patti Boyd Harrison, Marianne Faithfull, Anita Pallenberg and the other '60s girls were themselves responsible for a new, watered-down retail image (the dolly bird) – and again it was feminine rather than *female* . . . a fragile, vulnerable image of extreme youth, all wide eyes and long legs. The Romantic heritage at last ripe for seduction (thanks to the Pill), but still built on banks of commercially promoted accessories, from Yardley make-up to pale-hued pantyhose – all required for the Swinging style.

The late '60s brought what parents had always feared from rock and roll: a youth apocalypse. It was fuelled and symbolised by the release and defiance, the exhibitionism and autonomy of two things – the drug experience and a music which had evolved from pop into a hard rock which utilised massive amplification and exploited to the full its celebration of sex, dope and self-expression. It offered a synthesis of product and promise to a generation who had never known a non-electric culture. And it gave female rock fans their most pivotal figure so far – Janis Joplin.

The first major style and fashion changes of the psychedelic era had filtered out of San Francisco. They were the product of that enduring Beatnik myth which had been absent from media consciousness until San Francisco's North Beach bohemians migrated to the Haight-Ashbury district, where the ecstatic community they developed centred around drug use, promiscuity, and – above-all – music which epitomised the scene. Their striking and singular clothing (much of it fished out of secondhand stores by impoverished but imaginative hippies) seemed in its juxtapositions to

explore the mythic possibilities of many points in time, from the Old West to the Victorian era. Fantasy and role-playing flourished: ethnic, craftsy and thrift-shop costumes all joined forces. Exhibitionistic and evocative, the clothes paraded themselves in the new ballroom dance halls – at live concerts which served as a stage for rogue-dandy fashions and for the assimilation of radical politics into rock. And, like the poster art which emerged to advertise these events, the ensembles showcased the flowing lines and rainbow colours which codified the psychedelic experience.

In September 1968, with the release of 'Cheap Thrills,' Janis Joplin – a woman – became the biggest thing in rock and roll. "Rock is the basic art form of the time," pronounced *Rolling Stone* magazine, "and Janis Joplin is the high priestess of the community."

Joplin was rock's first female *star*; her self became as iconographical as Mick Jagger or Jimi Hendrix and, while she lived, she was a presiding image of rock style in the popular mind. But most important of all were the actual precedents she set for other women who wanted to be involved in rock. She was different in every way from the persistent conventions of a popular feminine ideal: she had acne, weight problems, unmanageable hair and a masculine voice. One of her oldest male friends recalled Janis as "reeking of patchouli and covered in pimples – it wasn't until later she started getting into a more sexy dress bag."

Later, indeed, Joplin was able – through wit, style and sheer energy – to re-invent the whole idea of female rock celebrity style, and to make her version stick. She "invented her own beauty," wrote Ellen Willis, "just as she invented her wonderful sleazofreak costumes". As a white female, Joplin made a crucial new point about rock's potential for unbridled sexuality and she made it by establishing her personal conventions of rock dress well beyond society's own limits. Such clothing imposed its own rules: it was patently unacceptable in 9-to-5 situations, in offices, at sport, often even on the street.

As much as any male performer, Janis Joplin merged myths of stardom with myths of individual freedom and revolution. And her hip expressiveness, her outrageousness, was copied and co-opted by promoters, fans, pals, and – most especially – groupies.

When trash could become style, when rock could become the most powerful art form, all things seemed possible. And, like the life enjoyed by the early Hollywood screen stars, the life of Joplin and her ilk evolved as if designed to support the illusion of such freedoms. Yet Joplin died young and alone, and the long arm of convention nabbed her the moment she was gone, plunging her into the myth of the little girl lost, the ballsy chick whose act only covered a broken heart. It was a stereotype of the female rock celebrity which was to prove enduringly attractive to male fans.

As psychedlic plunder gave way to the overt theatricalities of glam rock, the straight world began to feel stirrings of envy for the rich and fashionable lifestyles of the stars and their satellites. Subscribers to *Womens Wear Daily* and the merging living-and-lifestyle sections of the press joined that mob of jet set rock groupies which could be traced back to the '60s pop world's predeliction for socialite connections. During the heyday of glam rock and that of its androgynous step-progeny disco, men as well as women were once more busy spelling out glamour as a serious business . . . with the result that designers and society folk of both sexes flocked to rock *as* fashion. Manning the façades, the music business faced off with café society.

Early female glam rockers with highly theatrical, gender-bending images (like Suzi Quatro and, more importantly, Labelle) assertively paraded amazing exaggerations of both costume and sentiment. And this came at an important time.

Rock judgements, and to some degree, rock consumption, rely on comparison and reference – and Labelle provided strong female competition to the reigning male stars of glitter-rock. Just as much as the men, they seized the impulse of the era to play with the approaches and images of gender, but they did it with obvious, larger-than-life humour and avoided the clinical notions of drag with which the male stars inevitably became lumbered.

Labelle's image was largely the product of two American designers who went on to carve substantial careers in the upper echelons of the rag trade – Larry LeGaspi and Norma Kamali. Designers like these brought tricks like trapunto and padding (first visible as a stage gimmick to enlarge the performer's silhouette during the heyday of glam) into the pricey mainstream of dressy retail fashion, dramatising occasion clothes for the Everywoman who could afford them. Princesses, models, actresses, the upper-crusty jet set and the well-off could all dress like rock stars just by patronising the right boutique.

But the social ramifications of glam rock turned from outrage to conservatism through the career of one group – Roxy Music – and through the gradual ascendancy of a fanglessly androgynous, slightly mutant music: disco. Roxy Music's stardom solidified the incursion into rock of the art

1975 Glamstar Nona Hendryx decorates her face beautifully for the stage. Photo by Mike Putland/LFI.

1981 African Queens: two of Fela Kuti's wives decorate their faces traditionally – for the street. Photos by Anton Corbijn.

school mob, those who applied to music a specific self-consciousness about style and a visual iconography garnered *outside music*, from fashion, film and art. Even more insidiously, Roxy Music were the spearhead for rock's unexpected new desire to perform as a *class act* – not just a sight for the fashionable to see, but a milieu unto itself as synonymous with glamour, pleasure and fashion as high society, yet with the added *coup* of hipnitude.

Because this new impulse targeted itself at a traditional structure (society), it relegated women once more to that structure's traditional role: the beautiful, decorative accessory visible in the succession of Roxy album sleeves and in the dress of Roxy audiences. These versions of glamour (very Art School pastiche) were constructed by one man – London designer Antony Price – and were epitomised by one woman performer: European disco star Amanda Lear.

A former workhorse for Price himself and a Roxy covergirl on 'For Your Pleasure', Lear became something of a female Bryan Ferry: re-asserting the high society image of female stardom – chic, skilled and untouchable. Hers is an image tailored with both the finesse of a modern Oscar Wilde and the steely acumen of a multi-national businessman, and tailored around the classic, continental version of glamour which dresses more in the mythic clichés of the heterosexual encounter than in mere clothes.

Names matter, choices count; that was the message of the Roxy woman. On Lear, as on other Roxy models and rock

star-socialite girlfriends like Jerry Hall, Marie Helvin and Bianca Jagger, Fiorucci could equal feminine wiles; Blahnik could stand for blasé worldliness; Givenchy for glamour and Albini for ambiance. Roxy re-made and re-modelled a whole set of popular assumptions about wealth, winning and life in the fast lane – and these were exploited to the hilt by the rag trade, from Barbara Hulanicki's Biba label to the most downmarket dazzle of anything advertised as disco wear.

By late '75 and early '76, however, certain segments of rock's traditional audience (the young and energetic) had grown bored with offerings limited to ageing rock Tsars and glitterati. Harder times in both the US and UK also meant that an entire generation of musicians, fans, writers, hustlers, fashionmongers and other interested parties were offered less by the music business than they had grown up expecting access to. And the new movement in music, into punk, was rooted in their energies (particularly the teen and subteen sectors of the audience – or market, depending on your point of view).

The punk renaissance itself, begun in New York City and engineered in London by Malcolm McLaren and designer Vivienne Westwood (a prolific verbal dignifier of her punk couture collections for a small shop on the Kings Road), fed on various earlier phenomena. They included the apocalyptic performance ethics of the '60s revolutionary bands (many of whose veterans became inspirations and participants again), the plagiaristic, ever-popular Bowie, and

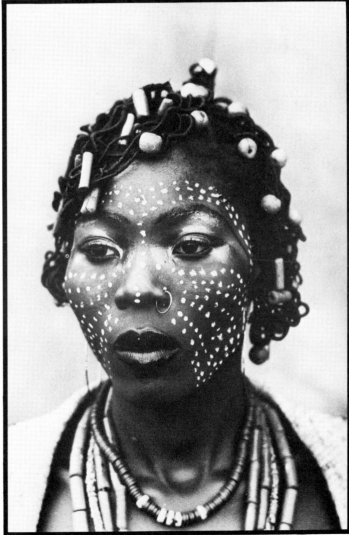

As years go by – Marianne Faithfull: There's a 16 year span between these two pictures. 1964: the shy convent girl poses for a photo session with David Wedgbury/Decca Records, with only a hint of her sexuality emerging.

1980: behind her a life as good-girl-gone-wrong. Rolling Stone mistress, druggy, serious actress and punk singer – Pennie Smith's photo shows a world worn and worldly figure.

a post glam rock posiness partly traceable to the short-lived New York Dolls.

The media ascendancy of The Sex Pistols finally provided some focus for a movement, and an entire subculture (with star system) developed from there. Its fashions and their stance were disseminated at live gigs, through an alternative press of fanzines, and via the rejuvenated publicity importance of poster art, sleeve designs and singles bags.

Because punk was receiving such massive mainstream media coverage, everyone had some idea of punk fashion as an entity: multi-coloured, peroxided hair vaselined into spikes, threads alluding to anything which might intimidate the passer-by (a mass of S/M-fascist, gender-scrambled evocations, an epidemic of scrap metal in the form of chains, pins, zips, buckles and bondage), and a deluge of badges as in the heady days of flower-power. Leather, plastic, rubber and vinyl clothing shared the spotlight with garments from jumble sales and secondhand shops; and the leather jacket was *de rigeur* for either sex.

Poly Styrene and Fay Fife constructed their own performance costumes from aggressively synthetic, man-made materials – Lene Lovich and The Slits assimilated personae from a desperate rummage round the thrift-shop. Poly and Fay told women something serious about the DIY creation of fun and the possibility of lightheartedly criticising falling standards of mass production. Lovich and The Slits were saying something else – reducing women to caricature (Lovich's vocals were as cartoonish as her cumbersome get-ups) and demonstrating how they could regress to being cute Little Cookies, complete with childish tantrums and Lolita come-ons.

In both London and New York, however, the leadership of punk's fashion-consciousness was shared equally between men and women. And the two major female figures which emerged from its new vigour in the end became almost symbols of the two prototypes of female rock style.

Patti Smith came to rock a devoted respecter of its fashion roots – in particular, that dandyish strain of poisonous-flower chic (the it's-what's-unkempt-that-counts ethic) best personified by her hero Keith Richards. And in addition to a certain Jamesian fascination with European cultural history – particularly her favourite boys, the French symbolist poets, as well as her assertion that "the English are the best dressers in rock" – Smith displayed many specifically American qualities in both her clothing and music. The word pioneer often appeared in descriptions of her costume: a counterpart to her aims to break new ground with rock and poetry. It could refer to big sloppy hausfrau frocks teamed up with heavy, unlaced boots or to that aviator-in-the-bedroom look of the parachute silk, Army surplus pants and American flag T-shirt she chose for her *Rolling Stone* cover session.

From a worship of the French and Italian film actresses of the '50s came an appreciation of intense sexuality exuded through apparently casual clothing – something which appealed to Smith's egoistic, no-holds-barred mentality. Her clothing, contrived to seem uncontrived, was also meant as an inversion and an iconography. Its illusions of anarchy *were* illusions, but her own physical appearance subverted the conventional ideas of feminine beauty just as Janis Joplin's had done.

A risky, adventurous sense of adolescence was something Patti Smith re-experienced through dress and self-presentation. Like a teenage boy, she dressed cocky and body-conscious: tight rubber trousers hugging immoderately long and thin legs, and loose shirts revealing delicate Praying Mantis arms. Smith liked to mix lengths, too; a long man's shirt with a short man's vest, topped off with an expensive riding jacket and a James Lock bowler. Layer upon layer of cardigans, T-shirts, and waistcoats, boxing belt and knee-pads, alligator trousers and heavy boots – a sense of combat-readiness.

From punk starlet to glamorous performer, Debbie Harry moves from the denim and leather of her punk origins to this classic pose taken by Pennie Smith 1978. Ironically, it reflects the formal style preferred by '6os pop singers.

The scent of battle was not surprising, for whenever women rockers have presented any image of true deviance (submissive subteen images in groups like The Slits and outright sexual panderings *a la* Belle Stars are not deviant), the press have reached for their artillery. And all subsequent commentary proceeds along the lines of standard social assumptions: Patti Smith looked like *that* either because she wanted to be a man in the first place or because an unkind nature did not equip her to look more conventionally alluring.

Those critics who felt so threatened by Smith's non-passive style of feminine apparel would deny her any femininity. But by swamping her frail frame in large and essentially shapeless clothes, she deliberately accentuated her physical vulnerability and reiterated those triumph-of-the-will metaphors which so much concern her.

Deborah Harry, by contrast, began her career in Blondie as a living image of the unsung therapies of American B-movie culture – fashionwise, a parade of pulp-fiction goddesses from slightly ratty movie memories. The enthusiasm for comics, TV, sci-fi, novelty songs and Pop art as useful raw material was not confined to Debbie alone, but shared by the whole band. Blondie revived memories which already came secondhand and Debbie's clothes came secondhand, too. But they were always used for their power as gimmicks (the best-publicised early example was when

Harry came out onstage in a New York club in a white wedding gown and opined, "This is the only dress my mother ever wanted me to wear . . . we could never agree on clothes," before ripping it off and belting out 'Rip Her to Shreds').

Debbie enjoyed breaking the rules – wearing the short-short skirts which weren't supposed to flatter a curved petite figure like hers; flaunting the two-dollar dimestore shades and out-of-date accessories (Courreges go-go boots, Paco Rabanne chain belts, patent waist-cinchers and lace-up shirts) and tacky Woolworth's fabrics. It took the mickey out of glamour to parade all one's images of it in rayon, acrylic, lurex and nylon – cheap lamé and leather-look; quickly Debbie was riding the crest of New Wave fashion and her

Take me to the modern ballet: The Slits stage their own fashion show for photographer Pennie Smith. Real '70s stylists post-punk, their dress is an excellent combination of the street and stage, the '60s mini and the '70s leather and plastic. The fourth figure from the left is *not* Max Wall.

Pauline Black, formerly of The Selecter. Above: pictured onstage with the group in 1980 when trilby and raincoat were worn to disguise her feminity. Right: in a Coventry back alley. The picture conveys perfectly the style, culture and dress of a young British black woman in 1981. Both photos by Anton Corbijn.

inventiveness was copied by countless younger female front persons. Yet, in her earliest interviews, she had been explicitly frank. "The most important thing to me is making money," she told *Bomp* just after Blondie signed to Private Stock Records. "I'm older than everybody else and I've put myself in a position to be fuel or food to the public for a while . . . To me it's all just the game. I don't personalise that much of it."

But Debbie did set punk style. As much as Smith or the succession of media-made pin-ups who were to ascend after them (like Toyah Willcox and the star version of Siouxsie Sioux, whose bodies come in for consideration before any body of substantial work does), Debbie encouraged a taste for Doing-It-Yourself and an anti-design stance in fashion. But as Blondie mushroomed, Debbie found her consistent experiments with glamour condemning her out of hand. To the mainstream she became a masturbatory fantasy; to her original hip fans, the scapegoat in a band which had been destined to sell out.

Debbie Harry had intended to do something new in the old showbiz mould, and that was to demonstrate that sex is a currency which can be used for all sorts of humorous transactions, as well as to show how one could play with the inherited, Warholic images and icons of the mass media. Her response to the punters' eventual dismissal of her counter-cultural credibility was to inch a step closer to the theatrical stereotype of performance clothing. She asked a friend, designer Stephen Sprouse, to take charge of her public wardrobe. And he put her into simple, uncluttered lines which flattered her diminutive shape but were careful not to detract from the famous Face.

They were still amusing, inventive clothes which reflected Harry's sharp and slightly underpublicised wit – mini-dresses and mini-culotte suits, with a recurring theme of one bare shoulder; neat contrasts of colour and texture; Marlene Dietrich-style glitz. Everything is organised now, and Debbie's dress has a different and straight-forwardly grownup unity – that of the entertainer, movie star-to-be and cultural icon who pulls no punches about frankly setting herself apart from her audience.

Debbie Harry's own imagination has received little credibility for the amount of new life it originally brought to rock and to street fashion – in the end, it's only her superstardom which has rubbed off. Because of her success, the stage personae of other female performers have drawn far wider publicity and public interest . . . from the tongue-in-chic of The Tubes' Re Styles to the assimilations of the girl B-52's (frank but more innocent inheritors of the early Blondie fetish for secondhand gear, who embellish the end product with outsize, frankly absurd wigs and party wit).

Post-punk, the options of women performers have shrunk visibly – and, it would seem, *voluntarily*. Survivors of the New Wave heyday are mostly poster-pouting self-fanciers such as Siouxsie Sioux, Nina Hagen and Toyah, whose dress is specifically self-promoting to the near exclusion of their music. Their rock style either *is* the act (Belle Stars), or it makes up for the lack of act (Pearl Harbour, Cristina), but no more is it something integral to the music itself and anything new that music might honestly be trying to forge. The latter category seems reserved for truly innocent young groups like Dolly Mixture or frankly calculating hacks like Grace Jones. In between are the genuine idiosyncratics like Ann Lennox of the Eurythmics and those old hands who know the score with regard to images but just can't bring themselves to be consistent – like the Marianne Faithfull of today.

Career chic has achieved its true apogee of premeditation and separation from the audience with the tremendous commercial success of The Pretenders' Chrissie Hynde and the USA's Pat Benatar. Sisters under the skin, both Hynde

GIRLSTYLE IMAGES AS . . . S&M fantasy: Amanda Lear.

Sexuality: Tina Turner by Anton Corbijn.

Rock 'n' roll astylism: Smith by Kevin Cummins.

S&M futurism: by David Corio.

Punk feline: Manchester punk by Kevin Cummins.

Punk sexuality: Nina Hagen by Anton Corbijn.

S&M fantasy: Grace Jones.

Spider woman: Jayne by Kevin Cummins.

Groupie: Cherry Vanilla by Stevenson.

Desert Girl: Tess of The Slits by Anton Corbijn.

and Benatar choose to ape classic *male* rock role models: Hynde the foppery of The Kinks and a stage condescension where Jim Morrison's leathers meet Robert Plant's strut; Benatar simple, post-disco body promotion of spandex and high heels combined with Heavy Metal metaphors. Both dress as entertainers with a cap E; both offer showbiz with a cap 'S'.

Hynde wears ruffles with leather, lace gloves with a sawn-off jean jacket – a sop to punk's past juxtapositions pulled out of context to create the persona of a Star (as Christine Hindley of punk's Moors Murderers, she wore a "dustbin liner and black jeans" – similarly a means to an effect).

In common with many other female rock aspirants like Ellen Foley, Pat Benatar has always gone straight for the *traditional* rock appearance of stardom (for women: to look conventionally sexy according to the fashion dictates of the day) with no alibis and no holds barred.

Meanwhile, there are still the post-punk would-be famous fans and fashionables, left high and dry with only the merchandisers to lead them on. And the merchandisers – aware that music isn't delivering as it has before – are casting their eyes further afield without abandoning the pretence that their wares are still a full-fledged part of rock culture.

Vivienne Westwood's Persian pirate collection (World's End label) sees her installation in the Big Time of New York City store boutiques such as Bendel's, Bloomingdales and Macy's . . . the very same spots previously tamed by export collections of Zandra Rhodes' £300-a-frock 'punk couture'. And, with Claude Montana (who put leather and wide shoulders on the haute couture map) and his romantic musketeer look the rage of the April '81 Paris collections, it's no doubt only a matter of time before Ms Westwood is mouthing off again to gullible parochial fanzines about how Paris "ripped me off" (*ZG* '80, Issue No 2).

These days in fact, fashion is shoring up rock just the way a plethora of media is shoring up musical event. As in the days of art rock, would-be stars and designers seal pacts of joint promotion towards the end of potential publicity (Spandau Ballet finally got Willy Brown's Modern Classics label some notice for his knockoffs of uniforms, *after* London Weekend Television constructed a show which made Spandau Ballet). And a host of magazines court the idea of rock fashion in the form of specific promotion for specific retailers (Melissa Caplan, Simon Withers, Stephen Jones, PX, Axiom, Manic Panic, Swanky Modes) in order to shift issues (*i-D*, *The Face*, *ZG*, *VIZ*, the style sections of the *Village Voice* and *Soho Weekly News.*)

The problems for women in rock, and for their fans and imitators, is still twofold. Not only is it as nigh-impossible for a woman to control her musical career with any degree of independence as it is for a male artist, it is also a fact that most women still seem to need images for survival far more than men do. So, from the catwalk to the aisle of the local record store, they will remain immediately responsive to new style from the rock world.

And the purveyors of that style and those images – however much their influences on concepts of fashion and stardom should increase – will remain susceptible to all the entrenched glamour quotients of rock's separate strata: sirens, hipsters, tough girls, Girls in the Street, the avant garde brigade and the totally out-to-lunch bunch. These are, after all, indisputably almost the only means to that career which will *allow* a woman to make her music. And their recurring cycles are part of that modus operandi by which the whole vampiric show retains its Dorian Gray-style grip on the pulse of youth. For the true goal of fashion, as Coco Chanel once remarked, "is not to adorn but to embellish, and each time fashion reaches its goal it is young."

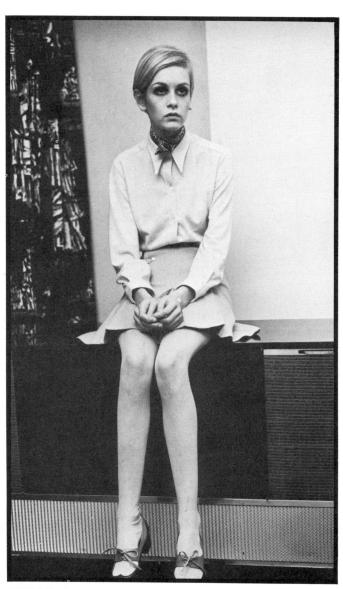

TWIGGY: To quote photographer David Bailey: "Twiggy was a spring flower child of the mass media; she opened the school gates to a whole new generation of models and matchstick women. Only when they come to evaluate the Sixties will the shape of Cockney Twiggy loom large and weigh much." Photo Syndication International.

JANIS JOPLIN: An intimate shot by Joe Stevens after her performance at the Woodstock Festival. Her style is one that inspired so many rock performers throughout the '70s and '80s. There were those who got down the drinking and drug abuse, but failed to capture the real essence of Janis' character. You either have soul or you ain't; Joplin had soul.

Nona Hendryx of Labelle. Photo by Mike Putland

Glam
THE VERY DREAM OF SMARTNESS
By Paul Morley

Think of glam. It's deeply significant whether you warm with memories of Roxy Music, a shiny shimmering example of an art directed existence, or despair at fractured images of Slade, deliberate illiteracy and scabby yobboism burying any embarrassing hints of bisexuality. Accept, if you must, the tired myth of glam rock – one of rock's more avoidable (punctuation) marks. Preferably, embrace the new myth of glam – the very dream of smartness, a metaphysical cloak draping all great pop music.

Think of glam. Chuckle at the genteel bad taste of platform shoes, the elaborate impracticality. Or respond to the cult of illumination. Glam: aesthetic heart or junked up joke? A harmless often hilarious segment of rock's curdling history, or a magically synthesising force that can elevate true adherents up towards greatness and even legend? Jobriath or Devo? Chicory Tip or Kraftwerk? Elton John or The Human League? Shock or Siouxsie? Billy Idol or Virgin Prunes? Sweet or Roxy Music? Steve Strange or Bette Midler? Spandau Ballet or Iggy And The Stooges? Duran Duran or The Velvet Underground?

Glam: the realistic cabaret condition in rock, energetically and gloriously relieving misguided sophistication and misconceived seriousness, or rock in painful drag stalling because of a lack of direction? A spent commotion or a permanent glow? Freddie Mercury or Howard Devoto? Naked Lunch or The New York Dolls?

Glam at its most commonly imagined is indeed glam rock: where opportunists, cynics, craftsmen, old men overcome a lack of imagination and crudely exploit glam spirit and inflate rock theatre to faint but fancy lengths. Think of glam and you'll switch to that period between 1971 and 1974; maybe you'll also consider the clammy so-called futurists of the early '80s. Glam rock is surface affectation: a cheap copy of ideal rock's inclination towards style and fury, gloss and lust; a ridicule of rock potentiality. I want you to think of glam and think of the scorching, generating glamour that propels the great rock music towards the intense point where it radically, realistically reflects the pressure and pleasure of our times.

Glam rock, as with most bald rock terms, contrives to cover just a fraction of the story. Why stick with it? The term tidies up a myth instead of unleashing new ones. Glam rock could easily get scored into history as the controlled, inconsequential antics of a handful of pop sub-visionaries and definite vulgarisers, points where pop gets too self-conscious and safely sensational. Where cherishable rock forces – the sex, spite, defiance, non-conformity, drama – are smoothed down and packaged to low taste. Glam rock, as commonly imagined, is a bawdy, joyless translation of a spirit – glam, because glamour is its base – inherent in all great rock music. Glam rock is another of rock's narrow and narrowing labels: one more hindrance to imagination, another slab of darkness cutting out the light.

Glam rock is a point on the map. Glam is the map. Glam heroes are rock's most profound philosophers, it's sexiest and most voluptuous stylists. They're prodigal, sensual, addicted. 'Blonde On Blonde' Bobby Dylan is glam. '57 Elvis Presley is glam. '67 Velvet Underground is glam. '77 Sex Pistols is glam. The beautiful Tim Buckley is glam. Glam, not because of satin suits and flashing socks and a lipstick smile, but because of a randy merger of chilling introversion, sacrificial extroversion, infringing presence and singular style.

Glam rock doesn't have heroes; at best it has idiots, rarely likeable.

Glam equals the finest possible image of what rock'n'roll can be Bette Midler is glam. She engages you in a furious intimacy and she raves. Glam is raving. Some do it more discreetly than others. Siouxsie Sioux is glam: compulsive, cosm(et)ic star! Glam rock is a masculine affair: confirming and inventing prejudices. Glam is common to no era. It is anything but homogeneous. Like Christmas and Heavy Metal it has always been around and will never go away.

Perhaps Quentin Crisp can claim to have pioneered the self-mocking rebellion that developed into the sensational and tragic glam. Crisp frames exuberant philosophy within perpetual and multiplying style; an enviable style. Crisp is sheer glam, and he knows why we're here.

In Gary Glitter you can see a faded creation of a similar, but never equal, consistency to Crisp. In Marc Bolan you sensed the same weighty optimism pinned majestically to an insidious charm. The glam glint in Malcolm McLaren's eyes is bewitching, and his involvement with successive glam heroes – New York Dolls, Sex Pistols and Bow Wow Wow – a sign of genius. From him you get the same twisting mix of allusive intensity and jaundiced instinct. If there is any trust, it is simply in the potential of the individual.

Crisp is the purest jewel of glam because he's long accepted that to serve sense to the brutal minimalism and injustice of life you have to look to yourself, transform a determined heart into damning art. He's decided that an expression of disgust and mistrust is most appreciable when the body is as sharp as the mind, when the shapes you throw and the clothes you wear don't contradict your moral and emotional commitment.

Quentin Crisp is glam godfather. He'll go to heaven.

Glam is the individual conquering. Glam is the ultimate display of oneself. Glam is a wholeness of body, mind and spirit. Magazine writer Miles Chapman once noted that Saints are very stylish. So Crisp and Bolan and Ferry and Midler and Devoto are Saints. True glam – to be the glamest – is an ultimate appreciation of the human condition. Clumsy interpretation of the spirit, crude handling of the raw material, can render it the most useless and numbing crumb of nonsense. Crisp proves that glam is an authentic solution: ideal style is effective resistance. Exquisite immunity from the tortures of society's trivialisations and trivialities, the heartaches and headaches of conventional practices. Glam is subversive and subjective, pouring soiling scorn onto conformist tastes and restricted codes, and for that reason alone an authentic ally of the truly wayward spirit.

You can find glam shadowing the most committed skinhead, creasing the pants of the most religious mod, melting all over the most genuinely outrageous Blitz kid, lacquering the spikes of the hardest punk. Glam is the spectacular embodiment of rebelliousness. A manifestation of profound disillusionment, of desperate discomfort with the cliches, tirades and expectancies of life.

True glam, of course, has an indisputable and unobtainable visual force: subdued like the all-black '66 Dylan, inexorable like Midler, classical like Ferry, precarious like Glitter. It matches this force with irresistible, even promiscuous intellectual grace. True glam is decisive criticism of emotional, political, philosophical dowdiness that implores us all to reject the ever-limiting regulations of our arbitrarily selected controllers, and mock the consistent condition(ing)s that mean to put us all in one place. It should be rational preparation, constant dialogue, broadening inspiration.

Glam is a series of coincidences. Kiss hid away on grubby New York bills beneath Ruby And The Harlots and the saintly New York Dolls, and then because of their agnostic vulgarisation of glam, they became the most popular rock group in the history of free America. Years later in English punk clubs, with walls sweating piss and floors ankle deep in

Left: Glittering '6os. Bo Diddley and the Duchess pioneer the true Glam image with gold suits. Photo courtesy of Thames Television. Above: Rod Stewart in a Bo gold suit. Photo by Robert Ellis.

1977 Another tour and another costume – sailor's hat and pantaloons. Photo by Anton Corbijn.

1978 David Bowie takes extravagance to the masses in Newcastle, UK. Photo by Kevin Cummins.

1973 Top: caught mid-flight between Ziggy Stardust and Aladdin Sane.

1980 Above: Bowiephile Paul McVey in his bedroom. His wife's name is Angie, his daughter is Zoe. Rock style influence at its strangest and most obsessive. Photos by Kevin Cummins.

Working man's glam rock. Superyobs Slade (Hill, Holder and Lea) at their
platform boot-stomping best – or worst. Delete to taste. Photos by Robert Ellis.

spilt beer and cider, Adam And The Ants stumble upon the glam spirit coursing through the comic inspiration of Lenny Bruce, staining the fart and then savour the smell of literate existentialism of Jean Genet, and bastardise it all within a non-glam punk strait jacket. They were so extreme and confused, and musically listless, they ended up as the creepiest of cults.

Then came a shrewd shift – from resenting anti-heroes, to a creative new pop confectioneering and a better if still afflicted glam version. Adam couldn't find much left to plunder in the 20th Century so plumped for a mixture of Red Indian, Pirate and Highway Man material. Malcolm McLaren helped him to style a commodious glam idea. Adam And The Ants emerged as the biggest selling pop group of the early '80s, glam idols to a new generation, a unit draped with easily copied accessories.

Kiss and Adam And The Ants served their audience well in times of stress. Theirs, though, is a muddy glam, compromised for the sake of acceptance. They find vast commercial success and earn the most faithful of organised Fan Clubs through a perversion of glam: acclaimed and accepted because of these compromises and inevitably trapped by them. They'd rather have spurious luxury than perfect their glam instincts! They'll pay later.

Adam follows Kiss . . . Steve Strange follows Jobriath. They both have a hazy understanding that glam offers salvation, but their attempts at glam are inept and undignified. Jobriath alarmed us in the '70s with a scandalously inappropriate expression of glam: all shell. Steve Strange then regales us with the crudest, in many senses cruelest, glam philosophy since Black Sabbath. He's an emblematic chameleon making few decisions and possessing indefinite direction: all dressed up, all made up, with nothing to say.

Strange's glam mentality isn't even as barely advanced as Jobriath's: he sees glam as a body that apparently enables him to elevate above ordinary mortals without having to exercise intellectual muscle or confront the realities which should form the nourishing core of true glam. Strange turns glam into something boring: as boring and joyless as a rock group. That's some hateful achievement. Glam should suggest a realistic, progressive design for living. Strange, like Yes, like Styx, closes you in, shuts out the light, fascinates you like an empty Fiorucci carrier bag.

Creative forces are important and natural, but not something to get obsessively serious about; serious in that you think about the act of creating too much, glorify your ability to do so, and end up so besotted with the thought of creativity you end up sounding pompous and souless. This goes for the non-glam Genesis as much as it goes for the glam Spandau Ballet. . .

They are symptomatic of the complacent, conservative elements in contemporary culture that pure glam explicity opposes. With Spandau you cannot feel that you're close to a magic. They're dour craftsmen working up a feeble glam froth. They dilute the drastic passions of Roxy Music with plastic passionless skill, whilst glam champions like Simple Minds and Magazine transmute those passions with propulsive vision. Spandau's glam is insipid and manageable enough to convince media dummies to help them into the hit parade and the high life.

Spandau Ballet attempt to revive and revise a glam version that was dreadfully mistaken in the first place. Spandau and Strange are approaching glam from a rockist viewpoint, for all their whinging about rock's offensiveness, and cannot survive under any reasonable scrutiny.

Bette Midler is always glam: saturated with prestige however painted and punctilious. Ferry is always glam: in spite of the puffery. Iggy is always glam: however much bluster. Glam is never consistent. Mud, tediously

Gary Glitter, back in the days when he could still pass for a slimline tonic for mid-'70s greyness. A showman at his peak. Photo by Mike Putland.

appreciative of viable commercial properties in those rupturing '70s glam rock days, decorated themselves in the tinselled colours of glam rock. But Stray Cats, troubled and vigorous, are a million times more glam. Jonathan Richman is more glam than Zaine Griff. Japan are trad jazz next to the glam of Fire Engines.

Glam's god Quentin Crisp would immediately sense the immense spunk in ex-Television's Tom Verlaine and shoo away the fake chic of Steve Strange. One is glam, the other despicable. One juxtaposes, contrasts, confronts and cultivates a classically erotic appearance, the other succumbs to an apparent pathetic fashionable celibacy. Make-up isn't glam: it's a small aid to representing it. In Crisp's own analogy – Verlaine is style, Strange is fashion.

"Fashion," says Crisp, "is a way of not having to decide who you are. Style is deciding who you are and being able to perpetuate it."

Ferry is style. Numan is fashion. Style equals glam, which can be prized as art that is in no way inferior to the technically complicated body that is usually accepted as art. Fashion equals glam rock.

Quentin Crisp, purest glam, is Art. New York Dolls, great glam, were artists. Cuddly Toys, weakest glam, were obscene jerks. Glam can be godly: glam can be the worst thing that ever happened to our lives. Glam is expressing oneself in order to be recognised. Glam rock is poncing and preening about merely to be noticed.

So maybe glam started with, say, Screaming Lord Sutch and Jim Morrison. The polarisation these examples immediately suggests is vital to any serious appreciation of glam, and to understand how glam erupts into glam rock.

Glam rooted in Screaming Lord Sutch is inarticulate, undignified neo-nihilism; a pissed up lark perhaps made funnier by its exaggerated accents and fancy dress. Glam rooted in Jim Morrison is the basis for co-habitable communication, a holy or perverse or magnificent or spasmodic quest for inner truth, the serious urge to reshape reality properly, to improve upon idealised style.

One is fatalistic, the other fatuous. It's both glam: neither could be casual or conventionally serious.

Glam is an historic inevitability. Glam is sweeping romance, an extravagant release of energies. All pop life is there. Splattered and splintered throughout all great music is glam's essential yearning for glory and escape.

Lord Sutch glam can be traced through to Slade, Sham 69, even Bauhaus. Jim Morrison glam can be followed through to Roxy Music, to Joy Division. Glam spirit allowed Roxy Music freedom to investigate and introduce the tones and temperaments of all manner of art and entertainment: stimulated one of the most importantly electric and artistically energetic musical developments of the 20th Century. Like the Velvet Underground, Roxy Music created unselfconscious, accessible and enhancing art/rock and did so because they were beholden to the purest glam spirit. This spirit considers no restrictions, and stressed that dreams and idea(l)s are as considerable a contribution to pop music's overall appeal as the pulse beats.

Roxy Music were radically populist: in 1972 they were the greatest glam group that had ever been. The cinematic scale of their visuals underlined that Roxy Music were dedicated, quite properly, to the synthesis of image and content: the poetry of style strengthened the inspiration of their art investigation.

Roxy were vital. With their best pieces of music, on their first two thrillingly packaged and presented Island LPs, Roxy touched and treated the emotions, they never abused them. The depth of their examination, the tension implicit in their music, their honouring of history and their determination to slide forward, is a testimony to the potentials of popular music.

Their representation of glam was especially refreshing because at the time of their cool emergence rock was grinding into an appalling, immature dead end. It was suffocating inside a non-glam post Sgt Pepper blues.

Musicians felt they could equal, purely through technology, the superficial grandeur of populist classical music. This was deemed rock's natural progression: facing up to its responsibility to grow up. These stupid celebrations hastened rock's descent into the dungeons of over seriousness, and stimulated a commercialised (glam) rock explosion. Oppressive technological-rock – Yes, Genesis, Deep Purple – was half accepted as being rock's avant garde, its stab at respectability, permanence and beauty. Even heavy metal groups rooted in the invigorating neo-glam tension of The Kinks and the special glam surrealism of Jimi Hendrix were disappearing into studios and mansions, distancing themselves from audiences, reality and any possible grip on pertinent art/work.

This was rock's progressive period: from the late '60s stretched into the early '70s. Progressive was a hilariously incongruous tag for a music, mood and manner which owed more to some diseased, puritanical view of life than anything visionary or re-inforcing. Glam rock was messy, quickly tamed but explicit criticism of this convoluted reduction of possibilities: years later punk rock, a desperate, intense, nihilistic glam manifestation, opposed and criticised the neutral numbing progressive rock far more dramatically and constructively. Legitimate glam despair can be our salvation from puerile progressive saturation.

Sex, style, eloquence, colour, romance, drama, dream, vision, soul, flash, intimacy, ambition: it was all being systematically stripped away as post-hippies adapted to business ways. The new rock order spited the spirit of Cochran, Lennon, Hendrix and glam, deluding itself and conning the youth. Roxy Music bought everything back in a flood. Roxy's great glam scythed through the pointless pomp and sexless ceremony that was striking teenagers emotionally dumb, and turned us on, up and through – visions of fancy, sweet desire, this is the time of our life! Roxy were glam saints; the noblest glam rock.

At the same time as Roxy Music gracefully broke through the rapidly enveloping rock boredom, Marc Bolan, with a radically reactivated Tyrannosaurus Rex, found a deserved and eventually popular fame with another of the most perfect of glam exclamations. His glittery and audacious T. Rex were one of the most magical, mysterious and important of pop inspirations.

T.Rex were as glamorous and as avant garde as Roxy Music within the context of rock's impotent slumbers: as beautiful and exhilarating an antidote to rock's joyless retreat. T.Rex were liberating.

As Marc Bolan journeyed through the complexity, tedium, triviality and horror of standard post-Beatles media boosted stardom, he maintained the definitive glam vitality. The value of Bolan spreads far wider than the surface appeal of the single hits: Bolan had a playful but limited insight into the rock'n'roll fundamentals. Bolan though was the catalyst for the curiosity of half a generation. The way in which he cracked open life's stubborn greyness sets Bolan up as one of glam's most inspired and inspirational saints.

In many ways Bolan epitomises glam, and was glam rock: there are the superficials: glitter on the cheeks, cheeky satin trews, leopard-skin lapels, gimmicky flamboyance, but also the profundity. Bolan represented glam as an ephemeral, vitally colourful entertainment and also as a force that can change people's lives.

Bolan loved to live and lived to love. This was at the centre of his exertions. His was an exuberant glamorisation: glam as encouragement. Ferry gripped your heart, engaged your intellect; Bolan almost comically sliced through rockist

Marc Bolan tapes a Granada TV show in August '77, shortly before his death. He took to punk, and punks took to him, but by now he was a lone cavalier in a new age of roundheads. Photo by Kevin Cummins.

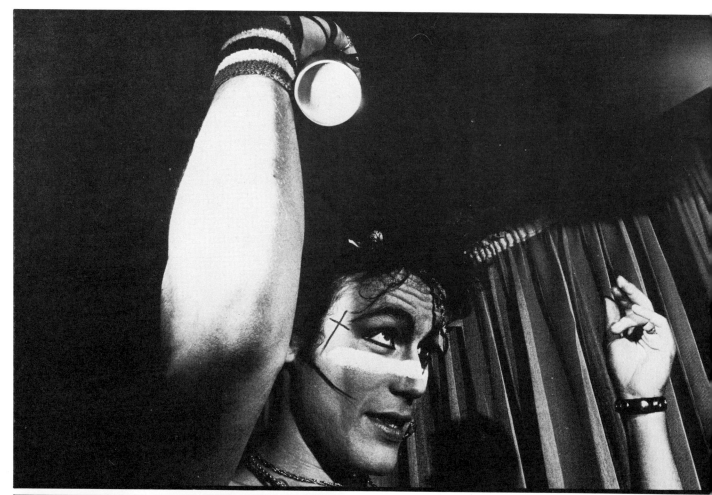

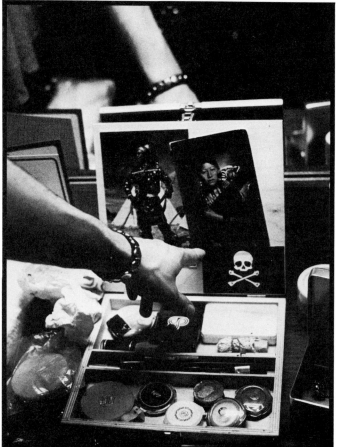

Adam Ant dips into his make-up box and prepares to take his 1980 tribal pirate roadshow on the warpath. Photos by Peter Anderson.

illusions of sophistry, of dreadful sophistication, and in so doing unleashed your heart. Thousands fell in love with Bolan and couldn't explain it. They didn't have to. And who would understand? Glam is a creation of new loyalties. As Steve Severin, of Siouxsie And The Banshees, has said: Bolan never actually said anything in his songs, or explained much, but his personal vigour and affirmations inspired us towards an appreciation of the finer things in life. Glam inspires intense response, is illumination. Purest glam increases the experiences: intensifies your appreciation of true and valuable style.

Marc Bolan fans formed groups of glam fascination like Siouxsie And The Banshees or Buzzcocks: those who thought Bolan was teenybop and risible went on supporting the de-sensitised grossness of Jethro Tull and Yes, maybe making way for Dire Straits or Fleetwood Mac, and will do so until the day they die. Non-glam inspired rock is a black and repressive thing.

In the early '70s – though few were properly appreciating it – Marc Bolan and Roxy Music were proving that rock music could still manifest itself as an irresistible cultural force, change the way that people think and behave in stylish and legitimate manner. Bolan and Roxy Music were as important as The Beatles and Bob Dylan. Years after, this could be clearly observed as Ferry style and Bolan verve-value shifted rock focus.

Glam's first tangible rise into view, as fad, as organisation of certain senses, had much to do with the rising discoveries of Bolan and Ferry. Deep dissatisfaction with rock's limiting service forced Bolan and Ferry over the top in their representation of rock necessities. They let their glam

tendencies explode on the canvas, overdid the visuals in their frustration at the dour and fading bewhiskered denim missionaries, the un-mysterious, un-mythical rock tycoons who desperately lacked the will to celebrate, even the desire to desire.

Progressive rock, from Led Zeppelin to The Eagles, was transforming rock into a cold, pragmatic, opaque collection of stiff styles and mystifying signals; abolishing rock'n'roll's metaphysical might, obscuring the grace and passion that addicts us. Bolan and Ferry sprang into action. They lashed out at rock's new denim dreariness and unsexuality by wearing irreverent, satirical, theatrical costumes, by making up and altering sexual codes, by exaggerating, worshipping and caricaturing the styles of the best rock icons. They gave glam an obviously, ridiculously glamorous face: sent up with great feeling and brilliance the theatre in rock and cinema. Out of their act of faith leapt a horrible mutation: glam rock, which crudely generalised and debased glam spirit. Their emphasis on clothes and appearance was ripped up and turned into a new, reassuring familiarity. A serious assault on rock lethargy was hysterically sapped by hard business hacks.

Glam rock became just another route to cussed success: a funny bright set of clothes to don, a uniform to wear in order to push formulised pop music into the hit parade. Glam rock at its worst totally lacked style: an astonishing turnaround from Bolan and Roxy's initial statements. Glam rock at it's worst was a definition of gracelessness; sheer paradox.

Glam rock, because it became so exploitative, easy, erroneous, because it was such a grinding, dampening adaption of glam and Bolan/Roxy's fervent favours, because it ended up so unfizzy, supplied many of pop's most hurtful and humiliating moments. Think, I'm afraid, of Queen, of Jobriath, of Hello.

You can almost blame glam rock on the lovely extremity of Bolan and Roxy costumes, on David Bowie's calculated caricature of the rudest glam principles, on Gary Glitter's shameless opportunism. Such poetic exuberance was taken and turned into a flash of gimmick. Glam rock became a rush of nonsense – The Rubettes; a rash of crazy, crazier, craziest costumes – Sweet; vulgarising cheap-pop – Mud; a joke – Alvin Stardust; a trivialisation of glam spirit – Queen; something that stood as proudly as it could for a mindless, mealy mouthed consumerism. It turned upside down the notion of novelty which Bolan, Bowie, Roxy were straining, divinely and insanely, to point out was an integral part of pop music. It diluted glam spirit to a point where only a small residue was left. Glam rock was a fad hardly worth noticing: relying on invalid shock value and a rotting sense of defiance.

Ploy and image was all: content all but forgotten. Visuals were deemed vital, emotional substance a minor consideration. In that first period of glam rock, up to 1974, The New York Dolls understood, thriving on a new tension between appearance and imagination; Sweet didn't. Gary Glitter, even, understood; Jobriath didn't. Here we come to what could be a classic misconception: that glam can be summed up by Jobriath's make up and Noddy Holder's mirrored top hat. Glam and glam rock are two different things, very tentatively connected. Glam is a guiding light. Glam rock is light comedy.

The Tubes, from America's West Coast, took Glamrock obsessions to the limit. Routines like this one, featuring leader Fee Waybill and his assistant Re Styles, were a ludicrous satirical gross-out – unashamedly over the top (or, in Ms Styles' case, under the bottom). Photos by Anton Corbijn.

Vamp Cramp (retired) by Anton Corbijn.

Glittering Ferry by Robert Ellis.

Freddie and friend by Kevin Cummins.

GLAM AND GLAMROCK IMAGES AS . . .

Ripper and victim.

Spandau in the works by Peter Anderson.

New York Doll by Joe Stevens.

Vintage loopy Lou Reed by Kevin Cummins.

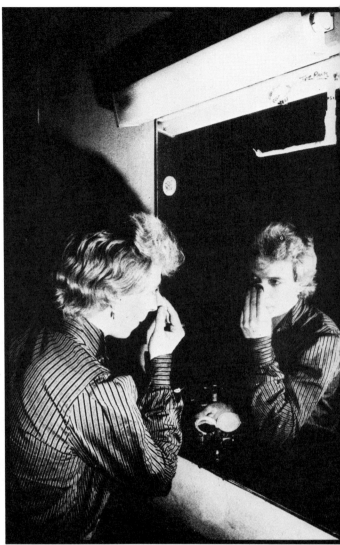

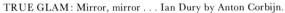

TRUE GLAM: Mirror, mirror . . . Ian Dury by Anton Corbijn.

Steve Severin of Siouxsie And The Banshees by Peter Anderson.

Glam is Sting singing 'Message In A Bottle' on a *TOTP* video, Marc Bolan sitting crosslegged on a Wembley Arena stage creakily crooning 'Spaceball Ricochet', Little Richard photographed eyes glancing heavenwards being pecked on each cheek by a starry-eyed starlet; Bob Dylan's corduroy cap in 1961, Johnny Rotten's face, Howard Devoto coming out with "*So this is real life* . . . ", Al Green's smile, New Order's 'Ceremony', Stray Cats' vanity, Fripp and Eno's partnership, August Darnell's suits, the dignity of Clock DVA's labour, the bass lines to the best Chic songs, Dolly Parton's wig . . . glam is shock, shiver, smile, scream, shout. Glam is: love that moment!

Far from being a liberating force that widened possibilities, glam rock restricted itself to exploiting attention briefly. Queen powdered over their raddled and strenuously serious post-Zeppelin heavy metal, playing along with the glam rock camp affectations until they were blue in the face and black in the heart. They emerged out of glam rock's sorry demise with a ludicrous reputation bizarrely intact, an awful image intact and pensions ensured. Queen are criminal corruptors of youth's desires. They adopted glam rock's commercialised properties to establish this thin image, flirted with bisexuality and are such a nightmarish representation of glam, so utterly unstylish, lofty and inconsiderate, they could well be the worst rock group of all time.

Glam rock preferred to be disgusting rather than dignified.

Because Queen and Steve Strange and Kiss bungle so lovelessly what should and can be a glorious route to transcendence they deserve our utter contempt.

One respectable compromise between glam and glam rock was Gary Glitter. He got pissed out of his skull exploiting glam costume but always retained an admirable sense of proportion and his best music had a vivid resonance that matched the joyful drama, if not the slight beauty, of T.Rex. His self-mocking attitude suggested he was faithful to glam spirit, if a little shattered by life's complications. His glamorisation was brash and funny, but there were always sad undertones. This sadness was compounded when a largely unaltered Gary Glitter got trapped in the early '80s glam rock bubble represented by God's Toys, Shick, Classix Nouveaux, the boys and girls in the Stevo stable, Duran Duran, Visage, even Ultravox. This glam rock burst was rashly and riskily tagged futurist. I prefer to call it fakerist: Skids' Richard Jobson, all glammed up with everywhere to go, calls the breed le Beau Monde.

The futurists/fakerists emergence in the early '80s parallels glam rock's emergence in the early '70s: ostensibly a rise up against pervading social and cultural drabness. The fakerists haughtily continue the tradition of such floating missing links as Japan, John Foxx, Ultravox, Doctors Of Madness, Be Bop Deluxe – units who attempted the difficult compromise between glam and glam rock during times (mid '70s) when fashion had turned right against them. And if in

Quentin Crisp by Anton Corbijn.

Stray Cat Brian Setzer by Peter Anderson. Well, who *is* the fairest?

the '70s glam rock had it's Queen, Sweet, Elton John, it also had it's Bolan, Ferry and Bowie. Early '80s glam rock/ fakerist has Duran Duran, Illustration, Visage but it also has Adam, Bow Wow Wow and Human League.

Forms of glam rock – commonly imagined early '70s futurist – succeed because in their perversions of glam spirit they appeal directly to the underlying needs of pop consumers. Because this is life and it's not meant to be neat and easy, glam rock Spandau Ballet will always succeed commercially, and glam Associates will be left to struggle.

Mott The Hoople were a moderate compromise between glam and glam rock: their hearts were there. Lou Reed even dipped his glam toes into the glam rock pool. Sweet were boorish brickies breaking wind in a posh public bar and trying listlessly to disguise the smell with the cheapest perfume imaginable. The foolhardy Steve Harley persistently pleaded that he was caught up in the beauty and terror of glam, claimed he was game enough to cleanse the crap out of rock's system, but his Cockney Rebel were just occasionally attractive pre-fakerist charlatans. Bumptious, virulent glam rock: weakest glam.

Slade padded themselves out in satin and that because it was the thing to do. Previously they were scowling skinheads, perhaps even the only real McOi. As glam rock piss artists they were a flare of fun now and then. Their bullying antics, ruttish projection, bawdy personalities and punishing good time music was the absolute opposite to glam grace.

Slade follow Lord Sutch and from Slade we degenerate despairingly through the crassest punk group (Pistols punk was incredibly glam; Cockney Rejects punks was glam rock) up to the ultimate in depravation, Splodgenessabounds. Elevation of the ego to the point where destructive tendencies are inevitable: the return to happy go plucky illiteracy and a panting pantomime representation of working class 'carelessness'. Punk groups in the '80s, who've turned over a spirit in much the same way as Queen up-turned the spirit of Roxy Music, can easily be shoved into the same way as Slade: in the '80s Slade themselves, appealing to the stagnant punk and heavy mental tribes, were dragged back into proverbial contention.

If you think of glam and you think of Slade you must be some kind of defeatist. If you think of glam and you think of David Bowie you're just a shade bit obvious. The revival of interest in Slade – a lethargic interest – is a terrible repetition of the sort of cultural desperation and confusion that fucked up Bolan and Ferry's glam perfection in the first place. Futurism/fakerism appearance suggested that commonly imagined glam rock is just one of rock's many genres that will spin and dwindle through cyclical motion until rock finally peters out seconds before the holocaust.

Glam can be that sense of soaring release that is vital in these nervous times: barely contained energies and the furious determination to attain perfection with the bitter acknowledgement that no such thing exists. Slade, Sweet,

Shock, Duran Duran: these people stand for conformity, for dull simplicity.

Without the erratic but elevating glam content of David Bowie, things like Slade and Naked Lunch could only be expunged with contempt. Bowie's maverick commitment ultimately allows space for all the loonies and the ludicrous: because we can find out how ingeniously the glam spirit can be conveyed the diluters get away with their stupidity. Bowie's glam vision, intricately and cynically articulated, at its most descriptive on 'Ziggy Stardust', troubled on 'Aladdin Sane' and anchored as 'Low' is the most acclaimed imitated and misunderstood.

Bowie through 'Ziggy Stardust' parodied and predicted glam rock excess, dealt with the sustenance of escapism and impudently defeated the rock dream. Along with Ferry's evocative suaveness, Bowie provided just about all the clothes and poses of the '70s glam child and the '80s Blitz kid. His works with Eno dictated the temperament of the electro-pop sound. His '80s nursery rhymes eloquently anticipate the most dangerous of times and carefully patronise the jumbling Bowie-shaped barrage of space imagery and space dress in early '80s glam rock.

Bowie's glam flair has enabled him to brilliantly transcend rock forms. He's a professional romantic, but a giant glam guru. David Bowie's single 'Boys Keep Swinging' is – along with Roxy Music's 'For Your Pleasure', T.Rex's 'Electric Warrior', Magazine's 'Real Life' and Siouxsie And The Banshees 'Scream' – the most scintillating representation of the point where glam seeps into glam rock: glam heart and soul vying magically with glam rock cabaret.

David Bowie has overshadowed both the commonly imagined bursts of glam rock: glam can't escape his shadow. Would it want to? David Bowie has been average, he's never settled and he's been the vicarious stimulant and actual genius. We can blame him for the new romantics, the futurists, the space cadets: we can thank him for inspiring the glam of Siouxsie And The Banshees, for giving sense to the glam of Iggy Pop. He's a pest and the jester and he's a Saint.

Glam rock is pretty prosaic. Glam is a miraculous, eternal substance. Think of glam. Alice Cooper or Captain Beefheart? Eyeless In Gaza or Josef K? It makes you think . . . Glam is independence, the reality of justice, full of incident and never incidental. It summons up your energy, sums up the times . . . a galaxy of myths, aiming to transform. I kid you not!

Glam rock at its best is never as divine as glam but never as universally dull as rock. It's a distorted compromise between the two. David Bowie is glam. Gary Glitter is glam rock. Jethro Tull and Rainbow might well be unamazed to hear themselves described as 'rock'. They can keep the label: it's come to mean something dried up and gritty. If Rush are rock, how the hell can The Velvet Underground or Bush Tetras be rock as well?

Think of rock: think of oppression, restraint, status quo, essential barrenness, a huge hairy con. Think of glam rock: re-constituted myth, a conjuring trick, perhaps comedy – when glam rock lost its sense of humour it was deadly. Think of glam: emotion, value, destiny, an understanding of and complicity with reality. Glam is a better word for what rock was always meant to be: it lends itself to all sorts of applications, triggers off the sexiest, loveliest images.

Rock has stopped dead. Glam is on the go. Glam rock comes and goes. David Bowie artfully announces that glam is this, that and the other. A spectacle, a demonstration, manufactured and discovered, artificial and natural. David Bowie, the Quentin Crisp of the 21st Century, has thankfully made clear the difference between the two extreme forms: glam and glam rock. The myths and the mirth. The very dream of smartness and the very idea.

1980 Pioneer electro-futurists The Human League play 'Rock 'N' Roll'. Somewhere up in heaven, the Big G looks down and wonders at the mutant sound he helped create. Photo by Kevin Cummins.

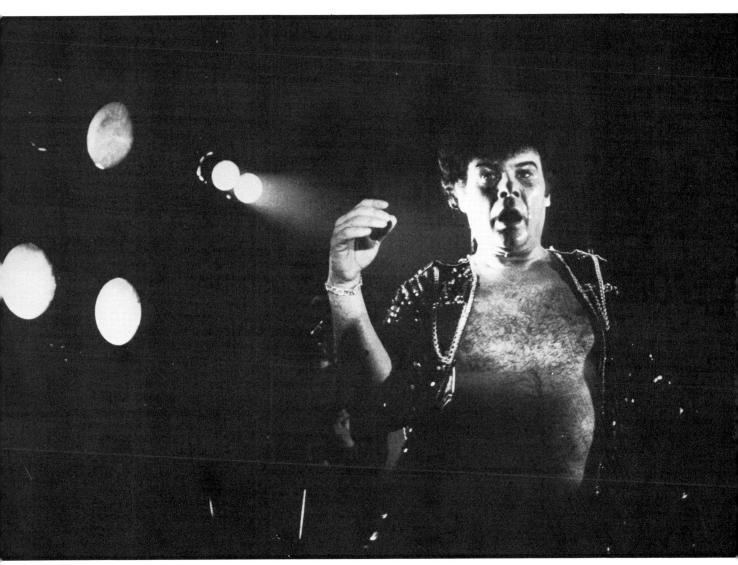

1980 The lure of the spotlight proves too strong for Gary Glitter, who embarks on a good old-fashioned showbiz comeback. Trouble is, there's far more of him to come back than ever went away.
Photo by Kevin Cummins.

Skinhead. Photo by Peter Anderson

The Seventies
REBELLION, REVIVAL AND SURVIVAL
By Paul Du Noyer

If it's true that distance lends enchantment, then it's true that it gives simplicity as well. A few years on and any decade can be wrapped up inside a neat formula, no loose ends, and so safely confined to history. The '50s, for instance, however they might have looked at the time, are now remembered as the rock'n'roll era, the first flash of mass trash, the age when teenagers were invented. And the '60s go down as the golden years of pop, the explosion of creativity that shook the consumer society.

But to make sense of the '70s isn't so straightforward as that, least of all so soon afterwards. This close up to the thing, it seems all trees and no wood. A confusion, a mess. Maybe passing time will bring us the perspective to impose some kind of pattern. And then what looks like the mad, meaningless movement of events in a thousand different directions will all have resolved itself into some orderly, logical form, ripe for a few slick definitions. Maybe right now we remember too much.

On the other hand, it could easily turn out that confusion is precisely the reputation that the last decade does leave to posterity. Very possibly the '70s will prove to have been the uncertain hiatus, the aimless marking of time that it was thought to be by those living through it. Rock music and all the appearances related to it, rock style, existed in permanent disarray. If there was any common theme then that was theft – or eclecticism if you want to sound smart about it – taking from the past to feed the present. The solitary stylistic innovation was probably the platform boot.

So what happened?

When Jimi Hendrix died in 1970, the hippy dream lost its last true flower, lopped off to leave some unsightly stalks and withering leaves. The alternative culture which had peaked in the late '60s, proceeded to die a lingering death. Most got out and got on, making the transition via hip capitalism or else matching flowered shirt and tie and a clutch of Moody Blues albums. A few others merely retreated from technicolour idealism; in dour denim, dug in to a sulking Underground, preferring to believe that time had stopped.

Even pop culture, the '60s wonder, was dissolving in a chaos of pessimism. 'Youth culture' – itself a term whose usefulness was doomed to obsolescence – never regained the fashionability, or the power and unity it had known before. From now on it was splintered and split. If there were no new confrontations as dramatic as that of the mods and rockers, it was because the '70s sub-groups were too far apart even to fight. They barely knew of each other's existence. The climate turned colder, media attention had turned away; reality was restoring its grip while the news grew grimmer.

Rock was foundering as a force because it had split along the most enduring fracture line of all, that of class. No wonder the more astute observers seized on the 1969 Hyde Park concert as a pointer: while Mick Jagger minced across the stage and his ageing audience, mostly college kids now, sat back affecting a sort of blissed-out complacency, there were young thugs up from the nastier end of town, skirting the crowd, tense and contemptuous.

The skinhead look embraced all that was ugliest and most opposed to the relaxed trendiness of a now-established and semi-respectable '60s style. It owed nothing to rock. Pop held nothing of interest to them – except perhaps for the then-despised simplicity of reggae and Motown. Mostly they followed football anyway. It took pop a while to realise

Top to bottom: Jethro Tull, 1970. Photo by Chris Walter. Bay City Rollers, 1975. Photo Kovesdi Press. Ant People, 1980. Photo by Peter Anderson. Right: Marc Bolan, Electric Warrior. Photo by Robert Ellis.

this: by the time Slade and Rod Stewart began to capitalise on the mood, skins had all but disappeared again.

In externals these new mutants were aggressively working class, taking traditional styles (big boots, braces, short hair) up to the point of parody. In fact it was the exaggerated uniform of an old proletariat that had vanished along with the blitz. But it emphasised that whatever future we were tripping into, it wasn't the prosperous and orderly planners' paradise so confidently anticipated since 1945. (Kubrick's visionary film of *A Clockwork Orange* was soon to depict this dream-gone-wrong in a vivid and – ironically – influential way.)

Optimism drained away throughout the '70s, as did belief in The New (as opposed to novelty). Obviously there were sound reasons, economic and political, why that should be the case. Tom Wolfe famously dubbed it 'The Me Decade'. Enough shocks were delivered to the system to persuade people that affluence and stability couldn't be taken for granted. Popular style simply reflected that. The overwhelming trend was towards entrenchment, to conservatism, revivalism and nostalgia. It was the opposite of the spirit of confidence and progress which inspired creativity in the '60s.

(With what was almost their last collective breath, The Beatles had ended the decade with a message for the '70s: 'Get Back'. The time for experimenting over, that chunk of fundamentalist rock'n'roll gave the word, and pop followed its masters' posthumous voice as obediently as it had copied their every move before.)

First of the new age idols to zero in on the situation was Marc Bolan. Sensing the vacuum in teenage life left by the development of rock into something older and duller, he turned away from hippy metaphysics and back on his own childhood inspirations. T Rex infused their sound with classic '50s flash and swagger, satin and tat, the cult of stardom. The brash glamour that Bolan created went on to define the style of pop for the first half of the decade.

Soon after, David Bowie and Roxy Music took the process up market, grabbing period references and outrageous imagery to produce a brand of glittering trash with an intellectual stamp to it that you could enjoy or ignore as you wished. Plenty of others adopted the glam ethic too, crassly and successfully – Sweet, Slade (after an early and clumsy attempt to identify with the skinheads), Gary Glitter, Alvin Stardust, Bay City Rollers for the boppers, The Faces and Queen for the rockers. The idea of the star was camped up. Decadence, however poorly understood, was elevated to a virtue. At the sophisticated end, it was a very knowing kind of fun. For the mass market, it was a reliance on an old showbiz formula for grey times: give 'em the old razzle-dazzle. *The Rocky Horror Show* celebrated excess with wit. A sort of morbid cult grew up around the legend of Marilyn Monroe, as if reflecting the sombre fatalism at the core of the whole circus.

Stage and street were never more visually separated. The distinction was rigid; glorified and revelled in. And as always, the style of the stars filtered down to the audiences: the Rollers' tartan, Roxy's elegance; at best the effects were dashingly extravagant, at worst the concert halls were filled with failed lookalikes – lanky, gangling Bolans and squat Rod Stewarts.

Even so, glam was never the whole of the story. For all but the most dedicated aesthete or intoxicated bopper, it wasn't a style that fitted comfortably with everyday life, with mundane reality. More than before, vast sections of the young population carried on completely unaffected by the dazzling sideshow. Pop might have been as noisy as ever, but it was becoming a minority pursuit. And meanwhile, in Wigan, they had Northern Soul. . . .

"*Here I go again! Here I go here I go here I* . . ." When Archie

Bell And The Drells began thundering out from the Casino club's speakers, it was the signal to spring up from the plastic chairs and on to the dance floor. Left deserted were the cheap tables around the side of the hall, surfaces sticky with spilt drink and filthy with cigarette ash, chewing gum hastily pressed underneath the edges.

While the sound throbbed louder and the strings soared and the beat pounded out, the lightshow flashed and the air was scarce. Learning to breathe excitement instead of oxygen, the dancers pushed themselves on to ever greater feats of daring, far from the clipped, disciplined little routines of earlier in the night. Back flips, hand springs, mid-air whirls, flailing limbs; skimpy vests, sew-on badges saying "Keep The Faith", steaming, soaked through with sweat, wide trousers flapping wildly; mouths open, eyes shut, short hair plastered down with perspiration. Manic oblivion.

And afterwards, the come down. Towels and talcum powder, damp clothes stashed in leatherette sports bags. Breath back, blazers on, three-button suits. Some soul obscurities on unknown labels changing hands for a month of wage packets. Out zombie-eyed into the morning, misty and cold, corporation dust cart trundles by. A milk bottle off the float. An hour's sleep in the bus depot. Breakfast, and then work.

And by the evening, when it was getting dark again, they'd meet up in pubs in Middlesbrough, in Stoke, in Blackpool, wash down pills with scotch and cokes, and it all started over. Northern Soul was 1972's only true underground cult.

Its whole language – secret sounds, soul survivors, keep the faith, the torch – was that of a sect. Historically, the movement was what remained of the original mods – preferring black music over white, obsessed with

This Is (Northern) Soul —
And Ska. Northern Soul was
the dance and dress style
that comprised back flips,
hand springs, mid-air whirls,
flailing limbs; skimpy vests,
sew-on badges, wide trou-
sers flapping wildly; mouths
open, eyes shut, short hair
plastered down with per-
spiration. Manic oblivion.
Cut-out figures and girl
dancer photos were taken
by Kevin Cummins at Wigan
Casino. Ska was a similar
trend, although the hair was
shorter, with sportswear by
Fred Perry; but the sounds
were black. Ska photos taken
by Peter Anderson at
London's Electric Ballroom.

exclusiveness, dressed with uniform austerity, a subtly-perverted restraint which stood in quietly defiant contrast with the gaudy rock-based excess that overtook mod in the south and finally became hippy. Overlooked, or forgotten, the style thrived in small, unfashionable provincial towns, hidden away.

The look helped preserve the cult's invisibility. To anyone else the northern mod's appearance would seem commendably conformist, or only mildly eccentric. The details only signified to fellow insiders: the vent, the turn-up, the right button fastened, the curl of the sideburn.

But bigger than any youth grouping, however, and even less indebted to rock, was the anonymous mass whose style was strictly high street. Period films like *The Godfather* and *The Great Gatsby* had their own influence; Oxford bags enjoyed some popularity, and the three-piece suit came back in a big way — investing the wearer with a certain facile self-assurance, they became the staple of the chain stores. Wide lapels and chalkstripe patterns emphasised the pre-modern, pre-'60s reaction. A figure like Kevin Keegan offered a model for far more than any pop-star, even if it was the likes of Bryan Ferry and David Bowie who initiated trends in the more cliquish circles — styles to be suitably modified for mass adoption.

By 1975, when the impact of glam was fully assimilated and its feverish vitality spent, another lull had settled. Vamps and gangsters were cliches. Biba's shut up shop.

For rock music in Britain, it was a time of creative stagnation. The old heavy metal tradition, personified by the megastar outfits like Led Zeppelin, lumbered on attaining even greater heights of overkill and tedium and elitism. But from one end of the decade to the other, it kept its tenacious following: almost entirely male, suburban, lank hair and logo-patched denims proclaiming an abject, feudal ethic of unquestioning loyalty.

The maverick Bowie survived by practically re-inventing himself from year to year: effete transvestite, sci-fi rocker, apocalyptic geurilla, American soulster, European aesthete, each new guise spawned a small cult of its own. But more predominant was the combined legacy of glam and heavy rock — often called pomp, this was the music of superstars and stadiums, a music which grew increasingly remote from the lives of its audience, weighed down either by simple conceit or by ludicrous pretensions, musical and intellectual.

Pub-rock, by contrast, functioned on a much humbler level: it was a tradition of localised, accessible entertainment, generally down-to-earth, gutsy rock'n'roll with a strong element of anti-fashion. Groups like Dr Feelgood — dressed like down-at-heel bank clerks, not much lovelier than their Canvey Island home, the exact antithesis of the 'dinosaur' bands — and Kilburn & The High Roads, and others, these alone seemed to offer any real vitality. Their appearance was pure jumble-sale, shabby and out-of-time, but at the same time it was the basis of a new style, one more in keeping with the feel of the time. The cheap, dated clothes suggested contempt for fashion and fantasy, paralleled in the music's stripped-down simplicity and hardness. It was an early warning of the next upheaval . . .

You could almost feel sorry for the flare-wearing foreign tourists that stumbled on the Oxford Street 100 Club in the summer of '76. Searching for good times, rock'n'roll and Swinging London, they wound up stroking their beards uneasily and staring in apprehension at the ghastly sight on stage: a shocking sight, an awful noise, and it was turning them and their rock dreams obsolete overnight. Johnny Rotten spat, sneered and screamed out abuse without discrimination, and The Sex Pistols' coarse, powerful sound galvanised a new generation of kids. Punk had arrived to dramatise Britain's decline. Its visual impact was even more explicit and uncompromising than songs like 'Anarchy In The UK' and 'Pretty Vacant' and The Clash's 'White Riot'.

Top: Wilko Johnson and Lee Brilleaux of Dr. Feelgood, whose no-bullshit R&B showed up the indulgence of early '70s supergroups. Photo by Robert Ellis. Below: Ron and Mick at Earls Court, 1976. Photo by Mike Putland.

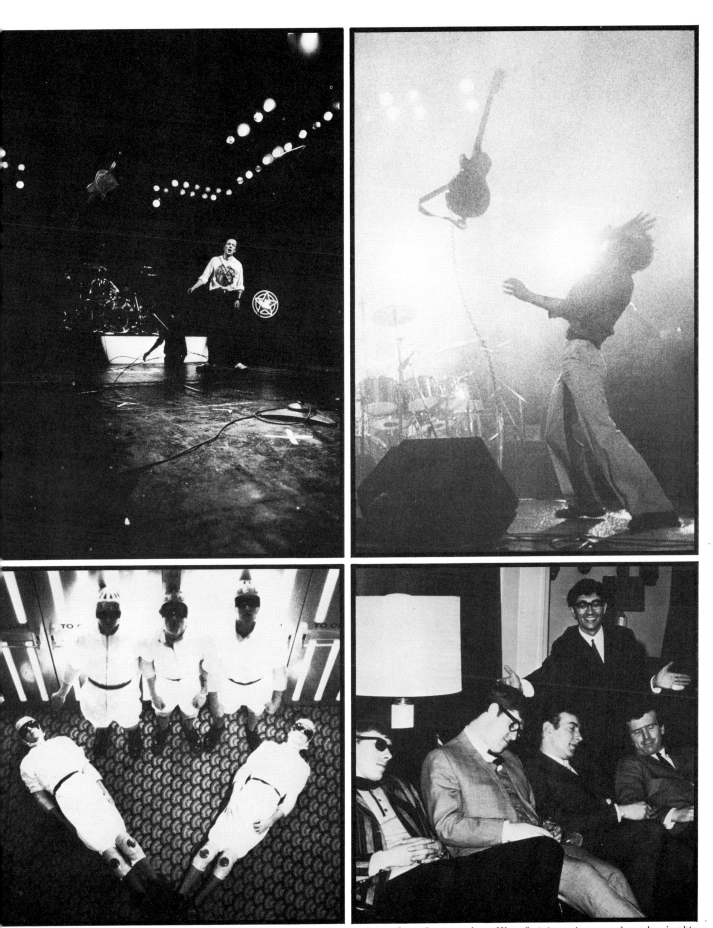

Top right: In this symbolic gesture, Pete Townshend tosses the magic guitar which confers Spokesman-of-his-generation status across to Joe Strummer of The Clash, top left. Photos by Robert Ellis and Pennie Smith respectively.

Below: In 1978 two members of Devo find the strain too much to take – just like Freddie And The Dreamers 15 years before them. Devo photo by Pennie Smith; Dreamers courtesy of EMI Records (UK).

109

WHY THE '70S HAD TO CHANGE. . . Clockwise from top left: Mick Jagger backstage with Liza Minelli and Raquel Welch, 1975. Photo by Annie Leibowitz. Rod Stewart with Britt Ekland. Photo by Robert Ellis. Ian Anderson of Jethro Tull. Photo by Pennie Smith. And Roger Daltrey of The Who. Photo by Robert Ellis. Right: Bryan Ferry, man about town, poses with model Jerry Hall. Photo by Gijsbert Hanekroot.

The Sex Pistols. Photo by Kevin Cummins.

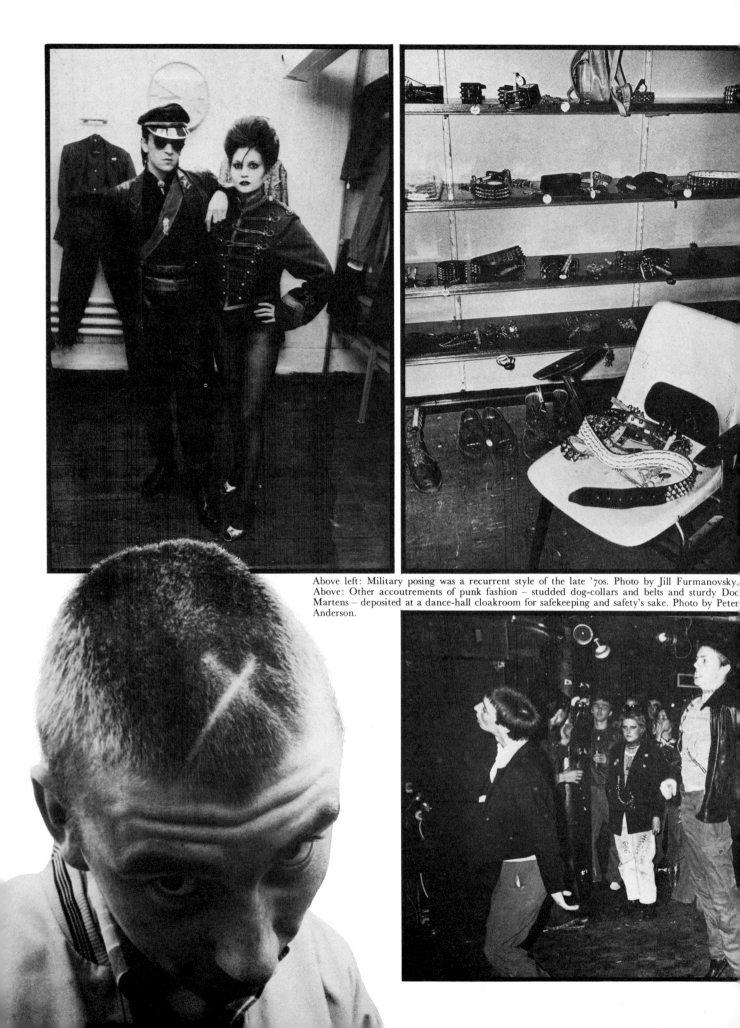

Above left: Military posing was a recurrent style of the late '70s. Photo by Jill Furmanovsky.
Above: Other accoutrements of punk fashion – studded dog-collars and belts and sturdy Doc
Martens – deposited at a dance-hall cloakroom for safekeeping and safety's sake. Photo by Peter
Anderson.

Above: the EMI publicity picture of The Sex Pistols, taken in November 1976 by Pete Vernon, which was widely used in Britain's national press. A dazzling photograph, it captured the Pistols' style perfectly, even if anarchy turned out to mean only an exploding can of lager.

Far left and above: '70s hair-care – Jill Furmanovsky's study of a skinhead and Anton Corbijn's zealous Jam fan. Left: London punks dance the pogo at Covent Garden's Roxy club. Photo Erica Echenberg.

Left: Vintage Johnny Rotten style. Photo by Pete Vernon, courtesy of EMI Records (UK). Top: Early Sid Vicious upfront at London's 100 Club with Siouxsie And The Banshees. Photo by Stevenson. Above: The Jam play London's infamous punk venue, The Roxy. Photo by Erica Echenberg.

Top left: Lora Logic (left) and Polystyrene of X-Ray Spex wear the plastic of a consumer society. Photo Erica Echenberg. Top right: Jordan manipulates her punky doll, Adam Ant. Little was she to know. Above: Early Banshees, more Glam than punk. Photos by Stevenson.

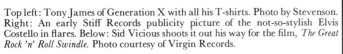

Top left: Tony James of Generation X with all his T-shirts. Photo by Stevenson.
Right: An early Stiff Records publicity picture of the not-so-stylish Elvis
Costello in flares. Below: Sid Vicious shoots it out his way for the film, *The Great
Rock 'n' Roll Swindle*. Photo courtesy of Virgin Records.

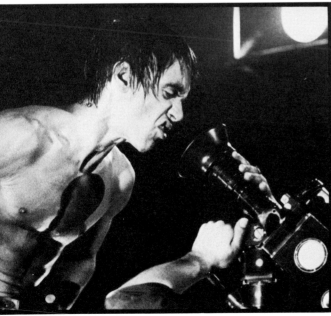

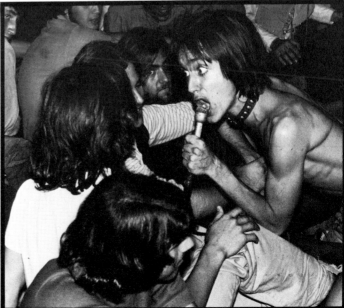

Top: The Clash trio as punks. Photo by Erica Echenberg. Above right: Iggy Pop in 1969, seven years before his time in dog-collar. Photo by Joe Stevens. Above left: Iggy in 1977, still without a shirt to his name and bug-eyed at his own film crew. Photo by Kevin Cummins.

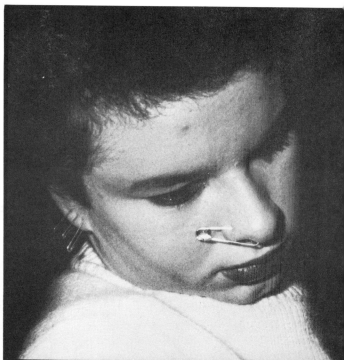

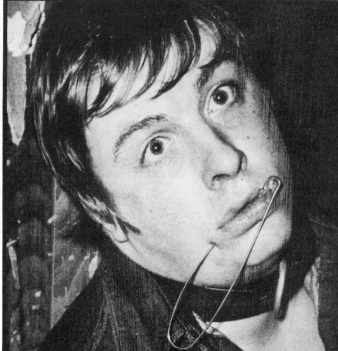

Real punk style: a combination, often totally meaningless, of school blazers, leather skirts, dog collars and safety pins. Far left photo by Erica Echenberg. The extremes of safety pin chic and pain show in another of Erica's photos on the left, and below the lip pin moron by Kevin Cummins. Below, another Echenberg shot of pinheads. Punk style was iconoclastic. Bottom left, fans take over Wayne County's Manchester show in August '77. Photo by Kevin Cummins. Below right: The Damned and audience share the spotlight in this photo by Erica Echenberg.

PINS AND PINHEADS

1976 The punk revolution will pause one moment while Johnny Rotten and his Sex Pistols have their picture taken on that very celebrated balcony at EMI House in London's Manchester Square where The Beatles posed for their famous first UK LP sleeve 13 years before. Glen Matlock, far left, was later dismissed from the Pistols for allegedly liking Paul McCartney. Going by this photo of Pete Vernon's, courtesy of EMI Records (UK), it seems you had to like *all* The Beatles, not just one.

English punk took some of its style from New York exponents of the urban nightmare like Richard Hell and The Ramones. But largely the look was inspired by Malcolm McLaren and his Sex shop, tucked away at the cheaper end of the Kings Road. The shop itself offered a potted history of the '70s: beginning as Let It Rock it took the '50s out of mothballs, then moved on to biker imagery as Too Fast To Live Too Young To Die. During its Sex phase it was the focal point in the formation of punk; once that movement was on its feet, designer Vivienne Westwood developed the look under the name Seditionaries. (By 1980 the boards were up outside the shop while Seditionaries was being supplanted by McLaren's newest vision.)

In appearance punk spelt chaos, collapse, catastrophe. In the desperate extremity which it celebrated there was a sense of negativity – of no future – but also of positive energy. Just as the music's adrenalin rush proved genuinely inspirational to people who'd given up on rock, so the instant thrown-together anarchy of punk style was idealised as self-expression and freedom from the constraints of fashion. (Inevitably, it's only a matter of time before anti-fashions are fashions in their own right.) While it lasted it was the most exhilarating time in the decade. With the possible exception of Northern Soul, it was the only movement of any great size which you could usefully describe as originating from the kids themselves. If the various industries – music, fashion, media – weren't slow to exploit it, in no sense had they created it for sale to a passive market.

In dress as much as music the ethic was do-it-yourself: the original punks took cast-off elements from all around and contrived a look out of them. Sex shop offered ideas and a range of images based on the central principle of outrage. Ripped shirts, straps and zips, bin liners and safety pins were all used and duly made the transition from symbols to cliches. Conceived as disposable, the various elements were adopted by the less imaginative as a uniform, and punk lingered on for longer than it should, but it's impact at the beginning can't be denied. The style combined anything and everything, from skinhead to teddy boy, reggae and glam, in one mad collage. Adam And The Ants traded on the fetishist aspect: rubber, leather, studs and chains. Poly Styrene of X-Ray Spex danced in the synthetic discarded

tack of the consumer society (and the message was 'Oh Bondage, Up Yours'). The Clash cut a dash with paramilitary swagger.

New wave—the glossier, more neutral term which came to supplant hardcore punk—swept the closing years of the '70s, its styles and its music advancing steadily from fringe status to the new orthodoxy. Elvis Costello's crumpled, sub-fashionable look—skinny tie, narrow lapels, short hair—got tidied up and brightened up for mass consumption by smiling, fresh-faced imitators. High street stores churned out the styles that the junk-shops had kept in circulation.

By 1979 the old lack of direction had descended once more. At one end of the spectrum spawned by punk, bootboys re-emerged in the East End and on the terraces: this time

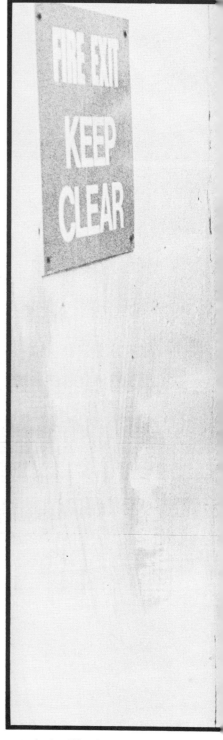

1963 The Beatles line up for the classic beat group pose that they were to use frequently during their early career, this time in a message to the readers of *New Musical Express*.

1977 Wam Bam Here Come The Jam! A in *New Musical Express*, May 7, 1977

around their preference was for the diehard stomp of the roughest, crudest, most basic groups. At the far extreme, cliques of art students, Bowiephiles and dandies were dressing up in the extravagant costumes of a secretive new elite, centred on the Blitz club in Covent Garden. Futurist or 'moderne' fashions enjoyed an upsurge, allied with the post-Kraftwerk electronic sounds of progressively-minded groups, many of which (like The Skids, Magazine and Siouxsie And The Banshees) had their origins in early punk.

Powerpop—a self-conscious throwback to the early '60s beat boom—was briefly in vogue during 1978, giving way to the Jam-inspired movement of mod revivalists—that scene

evaporated too, mainly thanks to a certain absence of internal dynamism. The success of Secret Affair and the film *Quadrophenia* provided neo-mod with its commercial highpoints. Somewhere between the mods and skins lay 2-Tone: a ska sound, a record label and a fashion with The Specials at its head. More earnest outfits like The Gang Of Four and the bands grouped around Rough Trade records offered yet another alternative: proudly non-sexist, slightly drab but often challenging.

Throughout it all, some styles remained perennial. Heavy metal flourished, with all its attendant conservatism (in sound and vision it was little altered since 1970). The

nnie Smith photograph for their first cover story **1981** To celebrate sweeping the *New Musical Express* 1980 Readers Poll, Anton Corbijn deliberately echoes the pose of Pennie's earlier shot.

country's student population, now more quiescent than at any time since before 1968, dressed and consumed music with near-complete indifference to the upheavals outside: the girls in their Laura Ashley smocks, the boys in their trusted cords and jumpers. 'Street' looks (street becoming the '70s cant expression *par excellence*) were adopted, with suitable modification, by those nostalgic for a time before age and affluence took their toll on lifestyle. Bruce Springsteen supplied the soundtrack for the hi-fi system. And above all, the high street ruled supreme, with Abba as its figureheads and John Travolta its disco gigolo.

Looking back, it's not so much a wood as a jungle. No

sooner were the '70s over than Peter York – in the January 1980 issue of *Harpers* magazine – offered the snappy definition of the decade's style as 'post modern': the time when originality came to be a matter of using the past, crassly or creatively, to form the new from a synthesis of existing elements. Maybe there's a ring of glibness there, but somehow it seems to make sense.

All that remains is to sit back and let those trees flash past before the eyes. . . . Let's hear it one more time for loon pants and grandad shirts, *Oz*, 'Alright Now' and Grand Funk Railroad, Ben Shermans, Nick Drake, Chicory Tip and Ziggy Stardust, *Cabaret*, stacked heels and feathered hair,

'Get It On', King Crimson, Black Sabbath, Barry White, 'Virginia Plain', Northern Ireland, "nice one Cyril", Sparks, The Rubettes, Elton John's glasses, Retro, 'American Pie', Habitat, Brinsley Schwartz, Vambo, the Fonz, the Jubilee, the Roxy, The Damned, Bob Marley, Grunwick's, Jilted John, *Saturday Night Fever*, Status Quo, Sham 69, Studio 54, Plaza and Johnson's Blondie. . . .

Sure, none of it matters all that much: style is a sideshow and too often its real soundtrack is the clatter of tills and the machines in a million sweatshops. At best it's fun – nothing in itself, not the real world.

And yet, to use an old analogy, it's like the petrol-spill on water: multi-coloured, complex patterns, endlessly changing, kaleidoscopic. Pure surface, of course, with no depth – but each movement of the oil means a shift of the currents below, something stirring in the unfathomable underneath, or a blast of turbulence in the air above. Where these cold winds – the real world – hit the mysterious, chruning sea – us, the human factor – there, right in between, you see style responding, in a million different, intriguing ways. And pop's where it happens fastest.

Pop fascinates because it's a shiny thing, and we're all big kids, we could look at shiny things for ever. Pop's one of those glistening, mirrored orbs which adorn the old ballrooms: not much to speak of inside it, but so polished outside. It dazzles: if there's a speck of light or colour anywhere around you can trust pop to catch it and throw it back, spectacularly. Only a cheap bauble, but watch it capture those reflections. Watch it long enough and it will show you your real world, in a myriad of disjointed glimpses. It'll hypnotise.

Pop, and pop style: always full of deliberate triviality and accidental significance. It may be dumb . . . but it can speak great sign language.

1962 The Shadows' great guitarist Hank Marvin begins to understand the meaning of Vox Pop. Photo by Dezo Hoffman.

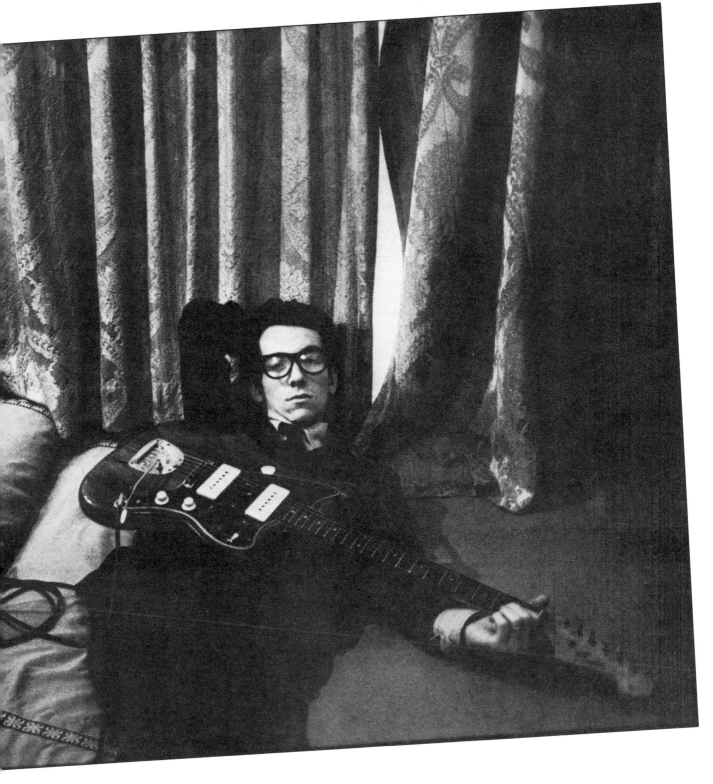

1977 Anton Corbijn's classic Elvis Costello photograph taken in a dingy hotel room in Amsterdam. "The room was so small I had to squeeze against the door and use a wide-angle lens to get him in. Few people had heard of Costello then, but now it's one of my most published pictures."

Top: Well, did The Kinks', Ray Davies devise 2-Tone or not? Photo by Dezo Hoffman at the *Ready, Steady, Go!* TV studios in 1964.

Above: The Specials by Joe Stevens.

Right: Dexys Midnight Runners by Mike Laye.

Top left: The original Selecter by Joe Stevens.

Top right: The Beat, a Go-Feet publicity photo.

Left: Nutty Madness boys.

SEVENTIES SOUL BROTHERS: James Brown by Anton Corbijn.   Sly Stone by Pennie Smith.

Bob Marley by Kevin Cummins.

Grace Jones
by Joe Stevens

The Eighties
FOR A LONG TIME I WAS
WITHOUT STYLE OR GRACE

Eastern promise: Sting in Bombay by Brian Aris.

The mystery of the Orient: George by Peter Anderson.

1980
The Clash and their shadows by Pennie Smith.

1960
The Shadows and their Shadows (who else?) by Dezo Hoffman.

MILITARY CHIC: Left – 1979 in the *Elvis* stage musical. Photo by Anton Corbijn. Above: the real thing, drafted and in Germany. Photo: Rex Features. Below: Bryan Ferry gets the GI Blues in '75. Photo by Pennie Smith.

Above: Another GI, this one's called David Balfe, once of The Teardrop Explodes. Photo by Bryn Jones. Below: Simon Topping of A Certain Ratio by Peter Anderson. Left: The full combat suit for ABC. Photo by Peter Anderson.

Headbanging comes back into style during the '80s. Grown men with long hair mimic their heroes, and they take their bedroom mirror fantasies into their own Heavy Metal clubs and concerts. Cardboard guitars and leather jackets with lots of metal badges are essential. Pea brains are compulsory. Status Quo ask: am I me or is he me? Who cares.

Photos. Top left: Mike Rossi of Quo by Barry Plummer. Right and bottom right, obsessed fans by Mike Laye. Quo, top right, by Sue Arber.

SPACE CADETS

1958 Marty Wilde by Dezo Hoffman.   1980 Gary Glitter by Brian Aris.

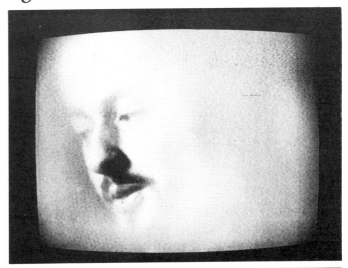

1980 Gary Numan by Dick Wallis.

1980 Space Cadet fans in Numan suits by Kevin Cummins.

1963   Little Stevie, the boy Wonder by Dezo Hoffman at *Ready, Steady, Go!*

1980 Still a Wonder: true style on his London visit. Photo by Anton Corbijn.

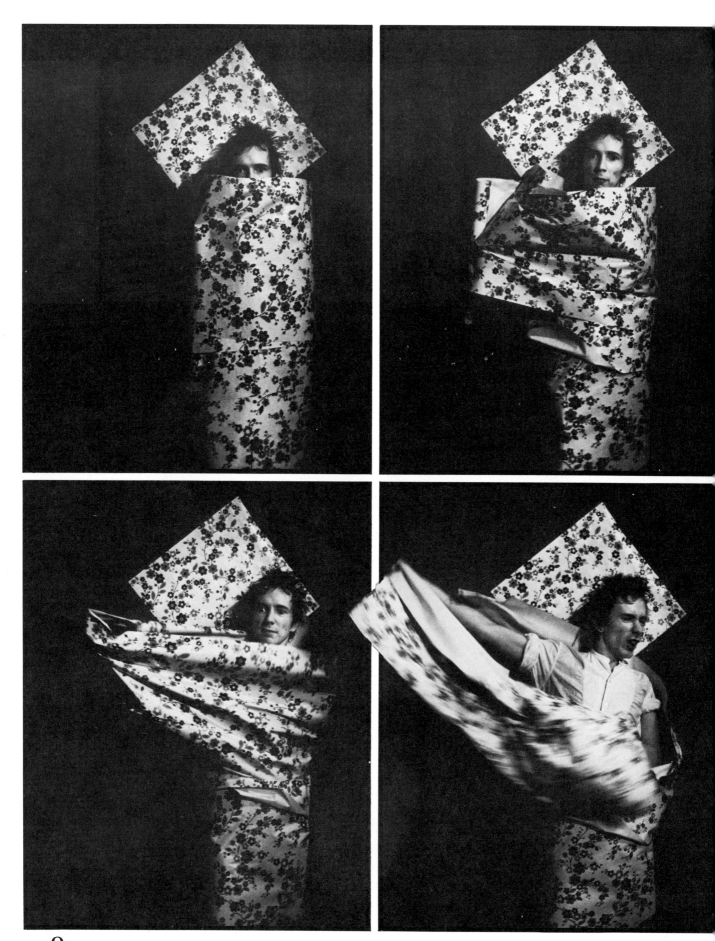

1981 John Lydon gets plastered and unwinds. Photos by Anton Corbijn.

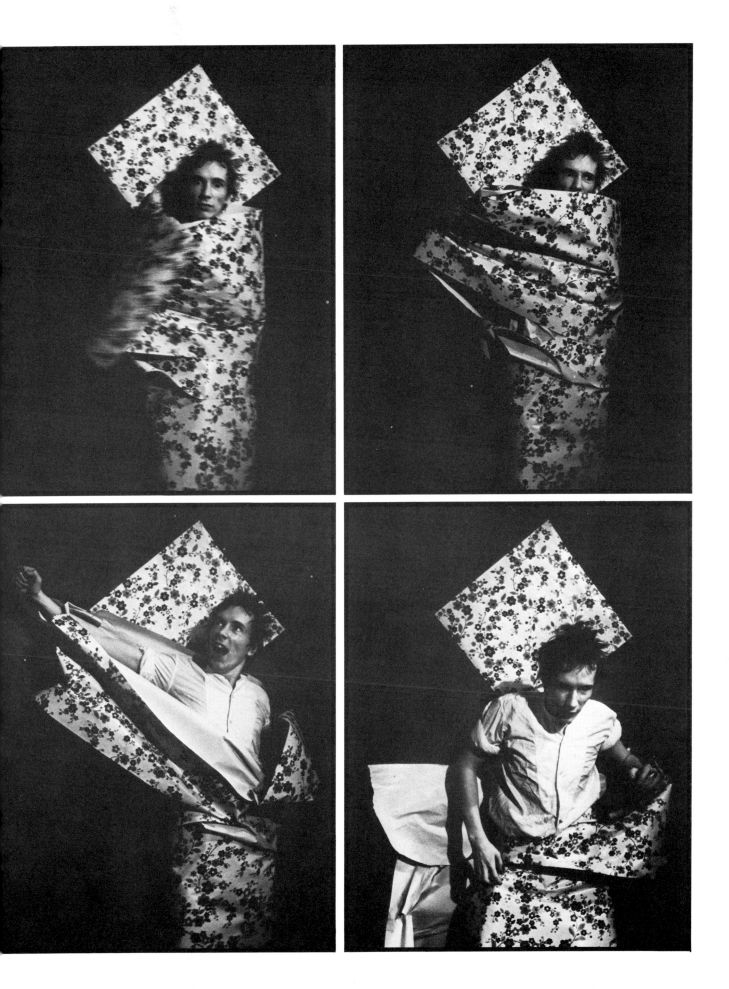

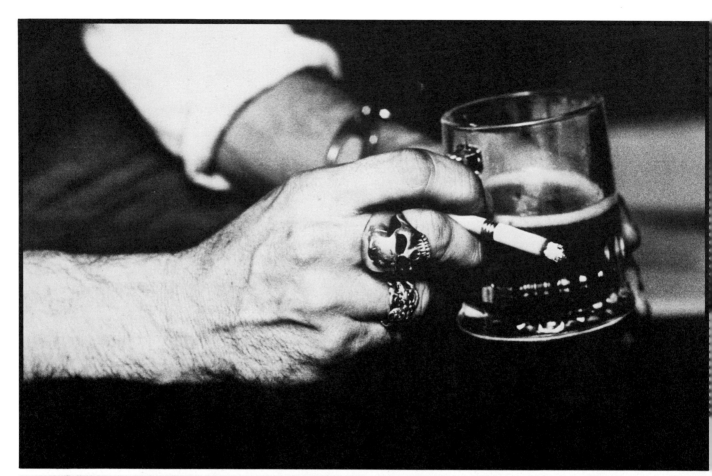

1980 You're either a pirate or you ain't – and the hand style is a give-away. Top: Keith Richard. Above: Adam Ant goes one – count them – better. Photos by Anton Corbijn.

1980 Adam Ant in full flight – a bizarre clothes horse of styles and influences, much of it inspired by ex-Pistols' manager Malcolm McLaren. A walking fancy dress party, pirates meet Indians meet Hussars – but it made sense to the British pop fans. Photo taken at London's Lyceum Ballroom by Peter Anderson just as Antmania reached its first peak.

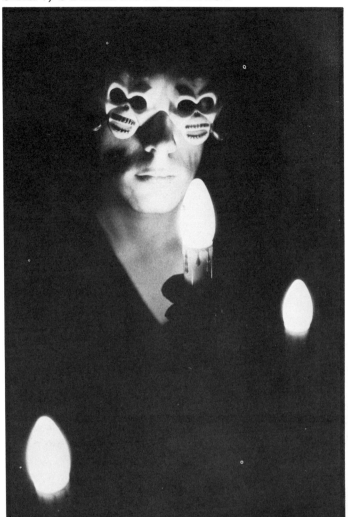

Pirate chic comes into style, but not unexpectedly so.

Top left: Anton Corbijn's photo of John Lydon shows his special skull glasses. Above: Adam Ant flashes yet more skull and cross-bones hardware for Peter Anderson to photograph. Left: Marco Pirroni, later to be a swashbuckling Ant, discovers eye-patch mystique from Siouxsie Sioux in 1976. Photo Stevenson. Four years later Marco asks, "Are you sure nobody's done this publicity stunt before Adam?"

Far top right: P. J. Proby and photographer David Wedgbury/Decca Records know the answer. Right: Johnny Kidd. Photo courtesy of EMI Records (UK). Far right: Bow Wow Wow get in on the plank, 1980. Photo by Pennie Smith.

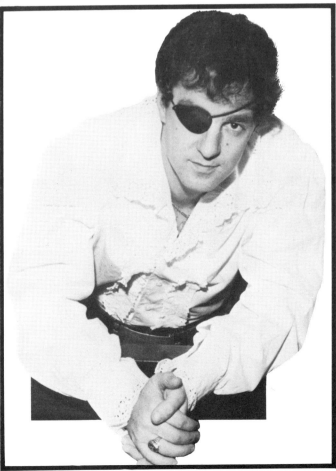

SOUND AND VISION
– PART ONE

1981 Vic Goddard by Peter Anderson.

1980 David Bowie in a Chicago bar by Anton Corbijn.

1960 Adam Faith by Dezo Hoffman.

1958 Elvis Presley by Lloyd Dinkins.

SOUND AND VISION
— PART TWO

Left: San Francisco Japanese Stowaway fan, helping the boom in portable hifi.
Bottom: Black Brit sound system at London's Electric Ballroom. Right: on the
streets of San Francisco a rapper fan. All three photos by Peter Anderson.

Below: Bow Wow Wow cassette piracy publicity shot, courtesy of EMI
Records (UK). Another trend to alarm the record industry was again master-
minded by Malcolm McLaren.

In May 1981, London's *Sunday Times Magazine* discovered The New Romantics and declared: "Lace and ruffles, ribbons and bows are all the rage right now, worn with jodhpurs or knickerbockers."

Left: Brian Jones, an early and tragic romantic, pictured in the late '60s. Above: A Manchester Romantic by Kevin Cummins. Right: Jeanette Lee of PiL by Sheila Rock. Rock style well ahead of the (Sunday) Times.

Annabella by Kevin Cummins

Julian Cope by Anton Corbijn

Ian Curtis by Anton Corbijn.

Robert Fripp by Peter Anderson.

The Lounge Lizards by David Corio.